MW00609197

THIS BOOK BELONGS TO

....

BE THE BOSS!

YOUR EPIC MONEY ADVENTURE!

GET WHAT YOU WANT!

BAREFOOT KIDS

Scott Pape

Illustrations by Richard Watson

HarperCollins*Publishers*

About Scott

Scott Pape is the author of *The Barefoot Investor:
The only money guide you'll ever need*.
It's Australia's all-time #1 bestseller and has
sold over 2 million copies. Scott was awarded
a Medal of the Order of Australia (OAM) for
service to the community and financial education.

This book is dedicated to . . .

YOU.

The adventures you're going

to have will be **EPIC,**

you just wait and see . . .

the ADVENTURE

Hi, I'm Scott
(but my mates call me Barefoot).

I'm glad you're here!

In the next few pages, you'll meet a bunch
of kids just like *you* who've used the steps
in this book to have EPIC adventures.

But do you know what's even cooler than that?

It's your turn now!

So strap on your backpack . . .
and turn the page!

Hi, I'm Betty.
I'm a working dog.
I love chasing sheep,
and I get paid
in bones.

I like the
feeling of
kicking off
my shoes!

Have you ever wanted to do something **EPIC?**

Like, say:

Buy a boat — and invite your entire family for a sleepover in it?

Or . . . have a $10,000 dog-walking business?

Or . . . build your own school?

Impossible, right?

Wrong!

What if I told you there are kids in Australia, your age, who are doing these things right now?

By themselves!

It's true. They're called Barefoot Kids. And if you turn the page, you'll meet a few . . .

Meet some Barefoot Kids!

“ I made $1500
from mowing lawns! ”
Paxton, page 84

“ I bought my
very own boat! ”
Maxy, page 133

“ I found $700 . . . in a bush! ”
Ava, page 98

“ I built
a school! ”
Amalia, page 152

"They call me the Slime Queen!"
Hannika, page 88

"I get paid $25 an hour to do homework!"
Matilda, page 90

"We turn trash into cold hard CASH!"
Ryder and Alexis, page 74

"I'm a TikTok influencer and I get paid $10,000 for one post!"
Tommy, page 96

Okay, let me guess.

Right now you might be saying to yourself . . .

'I could *never* do something like that!'

'I'm too young!'

'I'm not smart enough!'

Well, if that's what you're thinking, let me tell you about a 10-year-old kid with a **BIG** secret . . .

How Levi beat the bullies and became the **BOSS**

One day, Levi's teacher asked him to stand up in front of the class and read something.

He froze . . .

'The letters **jUmBlEd** up in different orders, and the words went into different paragraphs.'

He could hear some of the kids in his class starting to laugh. After trying (unsuccessfully) to get the words out, he slunk back to his chair and put his head down so he couldn't see the other kids. It was so **embarrassing**. He was eight and yet he still couldn't read.

After class, a group of boys cornered him:

'Why can't you read? What's *wrong* with you?'

Levi just stared at them.

'You are so **dumb!**' teased one of the older boys, and then everyone burst out laughing.

What they didn't know was that Levi has dyslexia (and ADHD), which makes words appear jumbled on the page and really hard to read.

So for Levi, the last couple of lines would look like this:

> worbs appaer jumdled the on dage
> and raelly harb to dear.

Levi was miserable . . .

'I felt like I was horrible at everything. Everyone was smarter than me. No-one liked me.'

And then a few weeks later something **weird** happened.

His teacher brought in a plastic ruler that had a see-through section in the middle. Levi had never seen anything like it. She called it a **'reading ruler'**, and it worked like a moving highlighter, which helped Levi focus on reading

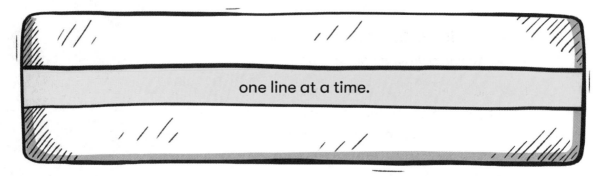

one line at a time.

The reading ruler was amazing! It was the first thing that had ever really helped him read.

That night he rushed home and told his mum the good news.

But there was a problem:

No matter how long Levi searched online . . . he couldn't find the type of ruler he needed anywhere!

Frustrated, he turned to his mum and said . . .

'I should get some reading rulers made and sell them to other kids like me who find reading hard.'

For the next six months Levi would come home from school and work on his business.

After searching online for ages, he tracked down a factory overseas that made reading rulers. He told his mum what to write in emails that went back and forth to the supplier, explaining exactly what he wanted and which colours.

He ended up ordering 25 samples to start with, and paid for them himself using his pocket money. And then he did something he never thought he'd be able to do:

He built his own website: My Dyslexia Shop.

Finally he was ready. He pressed 'go' on the website, and his mum put a Facebook post up to tell her friends about it. Then he went off to school. But he didn't tell anyone yet — he didn't think anyone would believe he'd set up his own business!

That afternoon something crazy happened.

When his mum picked him up from school, she said, 'Levi — you had 25 orders today!'

His eyes lit up . . .

'**OMG!** We need to get home straight away – we've sold out!'

The next day something even *crazier* happened:

250 ORDERS.

In the first two days he'd made $3000!

Because Levi's the boss — and it's all his money — he now tracks everything on an Excel spreadsheet.

He puts most of the money back into growing his business . . . but he did buy a professional remote control car (the type you race at a track).

And for every 10 rulers he sells, **he gives one away**.

'I give them away to people who don't have money to buy them, and also to schools. That way, some kids who may not have enough courage to admit they need them can try them out.'

Levi working hard selling his rulers

But the most epic thing happened a few weeks after his first sale.

Without Levi knowing, his mum had emailed his teacher and shared the business success. The next day, the teacher asked Levi to get up in front of the class and tell his classmates about his online shop.

Guess what happened?

No-one laughed.

Instead, everyone cheered and told him, 'That's amazing!'

One of the kids in his class bought one — and so did his teacher!

Even the kids who used to tease him were impressed.

For a kid who struggled with reading, he'd come a long way . . .

'I NEVER thought I could do something like this. But I did.'

Levi is a Barefoot Kid.

And he's just the first of many kids that you'll meet throughout this book. They're different ages and from different places but they have one thing in common:

they did something **EPIC.**

Levi thinks you can do the same

What you're holding in your hands is no ordinary book . . .

It's a guidebook.

What's that?

Guidebooks are what adventurers use to help them get to where they want to go.

And this book is YOUR guidebook.

This guidebook is going to show you how to get what you want. Don't worry, though. It's going to be super-easy — and tons of fun, too!

All you have to do is follow the SIX SIMPLE STEPS I'm about to share with you.

Are you ready?

I am so excited for you right now.

There's only one more thing you need to do . . . and that's to sign up for an epic adventure.

I am **READY!**

Signed: ....

Date: ....

Congratulations. You've officially signed up . . .

And you've earned your first reward!

I want you to turn to the back of this book, grab the very first badge, and stick it on the next page.

And then it's time for your first step . . .

to train your parents
to give you some
MONEY!

look for a sticker that looks like this

YOUR BAREFOOT BADGES!

With each step you complete, you'll earn a badge for your collection . . .

but, even better, you'll be one step closer to getting what you want!

Get ready for adventure
You earn it when . . .
You sign up for the adventure!

STEP 1: Earn some money!
You earn it when . . .
You earn your first dollar!

STEP 2: Stash your cash!
You earn it when . . .
You set up your money buckets!

STEP 3: Be a Barefoot Boss
You earn it when . . .
You start your own business!

STEP 4: Get what you want

You earn it when . . .

You save for your first purchase!

STEP 5: Make someone smile

You earn it when . . .

You help someone!

STEP 6: Grow your money

You earn it when . . .

You make your first investment!

TREAD YOUR OWN PATH!

Welcome

You earn it when . . .

You're a Barefoot Kid!

STEP 1

EARN SOME MONEY

We're going to begin this thing with a **BANG**

I'm about to show you the

fastest and easiest
way get some
money in
YOUR pocket.

This step puts **YOU** in charge.

First, you'll learn how to train your parents to give you money . . .
or a pay rise!

Then I'll give you a simple trick that will make you look more grown-up
and **feel much more confident.**

Plus along the way we'll answer the mysterious question:

'Where does money come from?'

(Oh, and I'll also explain why you should never walk barefoot
on my lawn.)

LET'S GET GOING!

Where does money come from?

The kids you'll meet in this book are different ages and come from all over Australia, yet they all have *one* thing in common.

They all seem to be a little more 'grown-up' than other kids their age.

Why is that?

It's because, unlike most kids, they don't need to wait around for their mummy and daddy to buy them stuff.

Nope!

They're the **BOSS**.

And they've worked out something that all grown-ups know: money comes from working.

In fact, that's so important let's say it again, louder:

Money comes from working!

Yes, money comes from working. If you want cool stuff — and you don't want to wait around for Christmas or your birthday — you're going to have to work for it. Plus, **doing jobs and earning money is lots of fun!**

Soon I'm going to help you set up your very own business so you can buy really cool stuff (like a Nintendo Switch or even a boat), but right now we're going to start small and earn some quick money.

How?

By getting your parents to pay you to do **three simple jobs** around your house.

Now you might be already doing jobs around the house, or maybe you did them for a while and then stopped. That doesn't matter. The plan we're on is different because . . .

You are in charge, and YOU decide the jobs.

Trust me, I learnt this the hard way. I let my dad choose my jobs, and it turned out very, very badly.

You see, Dad *loves* his lawn, but he *hates* dog poo (or, as I call them, 'dog logs').

'I'm going to pay you 10 cents a turd,' he announced.

And that was that. He'd given me my job, and it STANK!

I'd be watching television, and out of the corner of my eye I'd see our dog rock back on his hind legs and launch another 10-cent missile. Then Dad would yell out to me, 'Scott, go and pick up that turd off my lawn **NOW**.'

IT WAS HORRIBLE!

What's the lesson here? You need to choose your own jobs.

So let's shout this one out too:

DON'T PICK UP TURDS FOR 10 CENTS!

Okay, now I want you to go and
GRAB A PEN OR A PENCIL.

(Go on, I'll wait.)

On the next page I've put together a handy list of jobs that you can do around your house, that your parents will pay you for. Most of them can be done in a few minutes, or on the weekend.

Have a look at the list and circle **three jobs** you think you'd be good at (or think of some of your own).

YOUR PAYDAY JOBS

(no dogs logs allowed)

Younger kids
(up to 7 years old)

1. Set the table (or clear the table)

2. Help put the groceries away

3. Help fold washing and put clothes away

4. Help stock the toilet paper

5. Pack up all your toys and really tidy your room on a Sunday

Write down some of your own!

....

....

....

....

....

Older kids
(8 to 13 years old)

1. Clean out the car once a week

2. Put the bins out each week, and bring them back in

3. Clean up outside (sweeping, mowing, watering)

4. Feed the pets each night

5. Do the washing and folding on a Sunday

Write down some of your own!

....

....

....

....

....

The Thomson kids do different jobs around the house

Alex (5) is paid **$5** a week

'I make my bed (as best I can), help set the table for dinner, and wipe down the benches.'

Oliver (8) is paid **$8** a week

'I set the table for dinner, do the dishes, and sweep the floors.'

Isaac (10) is paid **$10** a week

'I clean my room, feed the chickens, and do the dishes.'

Ebony (13) is paid **$13** a week

'I feed the dogs each day, help with dinner, and do laundry once a week.'

You're probably thinking . . .

But I don't want to do jobs!

The most successful people in the world all have one thing in common: they're hard workers.

Remember, money comes from working. So if you want cool stuff you have to work for it.

Just try it for a week. It's actually pretty fun to do jobs . . . nearly as much fun as getting PAID!

But I already do jobs!

Awesome, you're already at the front of the pack! Keep going!

We used to do it and then Mum and Dad forgot about it.

Parents are busy and they have a lot of things to remember, and that's why I'm talking to you!

This is your book and your plan, and you're in control.

In the next step you'll have a money meeting with your parents, and I'd suggest you get them to set a weekly reminder on their phone so they don't forget.

I'm worried my parents won't go for it.

Oh yes they will (unless you decide one of your jobs is eating ice-cream).

How can I be so sure?

Because I'm about to walk you through exactly how to pitch this to your parents, so they will not only love it but will pay you good money.

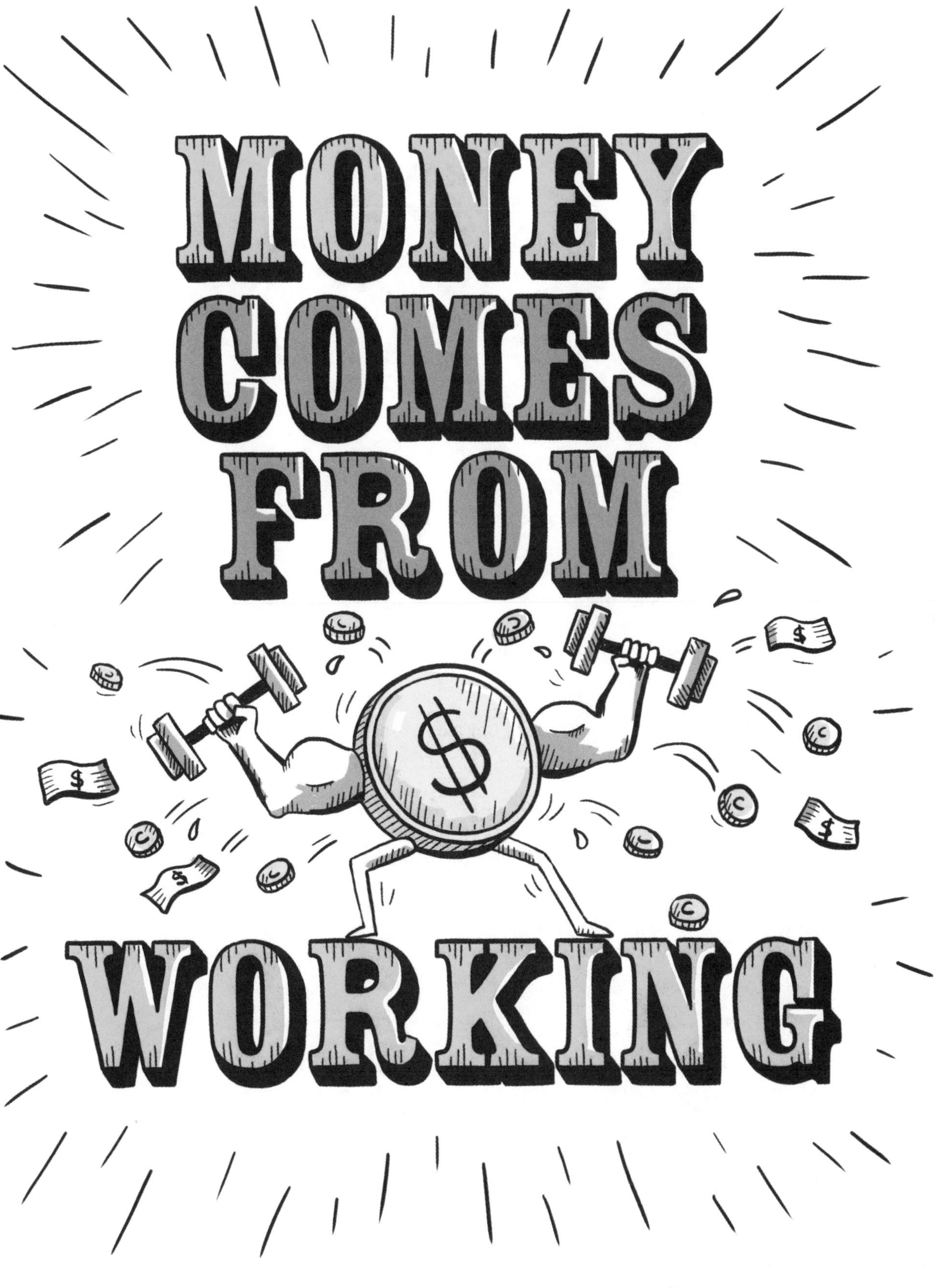
MONEY
COMES
FROM
WORKING

I can hear you. You have a **BIG HUMONGOUS QUESTION?**

HOW MUCH WILL I GET PAID?!

Ah, yes.

Let's get down to the nitty-gritty: how much will your parents pay you for doing your three jobs?

It's going to be different for each family, so you need to talk to your parents about it.

Some parents pay $1 per week, per year of age. So a seven-year-old would get $7 a week.

Other families pay 50 cents per week, per year of age. So a seven-year-old would get $3.50 a week.

And that brings us to a very important point.

Being able to talk to people confidently is a superpower that will get you what you want.

If I got paid in dog years, I'd get a $7 raise each year!

How to train your parents to pay you (more) money

Alright, now this is important. Listen carefully.

I'm going to share with you two skills that are going to impress everybody, including your parents. And if you're already doing jobs, these skills might just land you a **pay rise!**

Here they are:

First you're going to do something I call

'Parent Pleasers'

— they will make your parents really happy.

Then I'm going to show you a little trick that makes you look more grown-up and more confident when you're asking for what you want.

Let's start with the Parent Pleasers . . .

Happy parents = generous parents!

Your mum's VERY expensive spag bol

I want you to imagine for a second that you're really hungry.

'What's for dinner tonight, Mum?' you ask.

'You're in luck, we're having your favourite . . . spag bol!' she replies.

She places the steamy, saucy plate down in front of you.
Just as you're about to dive in, she sticks out her hand and says:

'That'll be $22, thanks!'

'You can't be serious!' you scream.

Okay, can you imagine if your mum actually did this?

She wouldn't of course — partly because she gets worried when
you're hangry (hungry + angry) but mostly because she loves you
and this is what families do: they pitch in and help each other.

This is the same reason you *should not* expect to be paid
for absolutely everything you do around the house. In fact,
if your parents are going to pay you some pocket money to do
your jobs, you really should also do some things just to help out.

Like what?

Like making your bed each morning.

Like clearing your plate after every meal (including spag bol).

Like putting your clothes (including your stinky socks)
in the laundry basket.

YOUR THREE PARENT PLEASERS

1 I will make my bed every morning

2 I will clear my dishes after every meal

3 I will put my clothes in the laundry basket when I take them off

Or choose your own!

Now let me tell you three reasons you should do these three quick, simple Parent Pleasers:

First, I guarantee you that within a week you'll just do them automatically. It won't take any effort.

Second, if you do these three things, your parents will nag you way less.

Third, and most importantly, your parents are going to notice when you start doing the Parent Pleasers, and be really proud of you. Trust me, this will help sweeten the deal when you start asking to be paid for other jobs.

Now let me tell you about another secret power . . . a little trick that makes you look more grown-up and more confident.

Barefoot the beetroot

Here's something I haven't told anyone, **EVER.**

I'm actually pretty shy.

I used to get super nervous when I had to talk to a stranger,
or my parents' adult friends.

'Say hello, Scott,' Dad would say, nudging me forward in front of
his mate.

And at that very moment my brain would go blank, I'd stare nervously
down at my feet, and my face would go red as a beetroot with
embarrassment.

It was horrible!

I was convinced that I'd *never* be able to talk to anyone other than
my family and my closest friends.

However, if you met me today you wouldn't know I was shy.
In fact you'd say I was really **confident**.

So what happened? How did I stop looking like a beetroot?

Learning to swim in the S.E.A.

I realised that talking to people was like any other skill — it got easier the more I practised.

Think about it this way.

Only a few years ago you wouldn't have been able to read this book, right? You would have been looking down and seeing squiggles and shapes on the page. Yet now you are reading about my beetroot face, because you practised reading.

Well, it's the same with learning how to talk to people.

In fact, I created a little saying called 'S.E.A.' that helped me remember how to talk to people:

S stands for **Smile**, which is the universal language of kindness. So the first thing you do is smile!

E stands for **Eye Contact**, which shows the person you're paying attention to them.

A stands for **Ask Questions**, like 'How's your day going?' which gets the person talking.

So when you think you will die from embarrassment if you have to talk to someone you don't know, just remember **S.E.A.** ➡

Jump into the
S.E.A.
Smile
Eye contact
Ask questions

YOU DID IT!

You've already completed the first step!

You know that money comes from working.

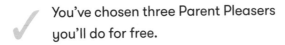

✓ You've chosen three Parent Pleasers
you'll do for free.

✓ You've chosen some jobs around the house that
you'll be paid for.

✓ And you've thought about how much
you'd like to get paid to do them.

Remember, every single step of your **EPIC MONEY ADVENTURE**
leads you closer to getting what you want.

❝ I'm the youngest so I do the tiny jobs. ❞

Alex

Alex might be
small but he is a
big Barefooter

Did you know that research shows that most people never get past the first 10 pages of a book?

It's true!

Most people flick through the pages, then put the book down and never pick it up again.

But not you!
You're already
way ahead
of most kids
your age.

You've taken your very first steps to getting what you want.

I want you to go the back of the book and get this sticker:

Stick it on the chart on page 22.

WELL DONE!

Next up, the fun really starts . . .

You're about to **GET PAID** (and you'll find out what to do with all that money!)

STEP 2

STASH YOUR CASH

Hold your drumsticks!

You and I are about to do one of the **BEST** steps in this whole book.

What makes it so good?

Imagine having **your very own treasure chest**, with loads of gold coins spilling out the top.

That's what this step is all about.

See, you've already done the hard work of thinking up three jobs you can do around the house, so now it's time for the really fun stuff:

 **watching the money hit your hot little hand!**

That's what payday is all about.

I'm going to show you exactly where to stash your cash, using my super-simple bucket strategy that will make you a better money manager than most adults!

Plus, we'll meet some Barefoot Kids who have set up their buckets and even opened their own bank accounts – they love being in charge, saving for their goals and always having money for little everyday things they want.

Finally, because you're such a superstar, we're going to end this step with a very special treat.

(Oh, and I'll also explain why you shouldn't iron your undies . . . or your $5 notes.)

Hot, crisp . . . cash!

My mum walked into the laundry and her eyes almost popped out of her head.

'SCOTT! What are you doing with the iron?!'

'I'm ironing my money of course . . . I like the notes crisp,' I said, as I pressed down on a $5 note.

She just stood there, staring at me with her mouth wide open.

'And then I store my notes in this little box . . . and *then* I pop the box into the freezer,' I explained.

'Is that so your notes are . . . cool?' Mum asked.

'What? No! It's in case there are robbers, Mum! The last place they'd look for money is in the freezer!'

Okay, I'll admit I'm kind of weird. Some kids love playing with LEGO – I liked ironing my money.

And if you think I'm strange, let me tell you about what the average adult does with *their* money.

I want you to picture a bucket.

Imagine that lots of adults put all *their* money into this bucket but . . .

the bucket has a H**O**LE in it.

So as they walk around spending,
the money drip,

　　　　　drip,

　　　　　　　drips out . . .

until they have nothing left!

Seriously, this is how most grown-ups manage their money.

And then they throw hissy fits about the fact
that their money bucket always seems to be empty.

'I never have enough money!' they whine.

At that point I yell at them:

'That's because your bucket has a hole in it!'

This situation will *never* happen to you. You are too smart for that.
You've got this guidebook to help you.

When you get paid, you're going to divide your money into

three money buckets.

And on the next page I'm going to show you how exactly how to do it.
No ironing required.

Your money buckets

Why do you need three money buckets?

It's so that you *always* have money ready to spend on the things you *really* want.

Here's how it works.

Each payday you're going to put some money into each of these three money buckets.

It's pretty darn simple, right?

Yep!

And by following my money bucket plan your buckets won't leak and you'll be a better money manager than most adults.

Seriously!

"We LOVE payday!"

Frankie & Poppy

your
MONEY BUCKET
plan

SPLURGE

SAVE

GIVE

EVERYDAY SPENDING	SAVINGS GOALS	MAKE PEOPLE SMILE
little things	big things worth working for	acts of kindness

RULE: Every bucket gets some money every payday

You're a buckethead, Barefoot!

Okay, let me get one thing clear:

I am *not* saying you need to use plastic buckets that your mum puts beside your bed when you're going to spew.

That would be kind of weird (even for me!).

Money buckets are just a simple way to think about where your money goes.

Instead of an actual bucket, you're going to keep your money in **jars**, or **envelopes** or perhaps in **a bank account** (see page 59). Let's look at how Oscar does it.

How my buckets work
by Oscar

AGE: **8**

WHERE: **Victoria**

My mum pays me $7 a week for doing my three jobs. Splitting my money into three buckets means I always have money for the stuff I want!

My favourite thing to **SPLURGE** on is Pokémon cards!

I did extra jobs around the house and bought a really cool Bakugan with the money in my **SAVE** jar.

I use my **GIVE** jar to give money to poor people on the street so they can buy food and blankets.

You're about to do something  **HUGE**

I have to say, I'm super impressed with you.

By sticking with me this far you are absolutely *smashing* it.

✓ You've chosen three Payday Jobs that you can do around the house (see page 31).

✓ You've got your three Parent Pleasers (see page 39).

✓ And you've just learnt the single best way in the universe to manage your money: three money buckets.

I think you're almost ready . . .

On the next page I've prepared something for you:

You're going to fill out a form and then all that's left for you to do is to sit down with your parents and

freak them out
in a good way!

Pitching to your parents

I want to start earning my own money — and that means doing jobs, because money comes from working!

I'll also do these **three Parent Pleasers** without being paid, because I'm part of the family:

1. ....

2. ....

3. ....

The three Payday Jobs I'd like to do are:

1. ....

2. ....

3. ....

THIS IS WHERE THE APPROVED STICKER WILL GO.

If I do my jobs, I will get paid:

$ .... per week*

Here are my three buckets where I'll divide my money:

Once you've presented your pitch this is what usually happens:

'It worked!'

'Told you it would!'

Go to the back of the book and find the **APPROVED** sticker. Stick it on your pitch.

look for a sticker that looks like this ⟍

'But how will I get paid? And what will I use for my three money buckets?

Your parents are probably asking the same questions.

On the next page you'll meet two different families who share how they handle payday in real life.

Our parents pay us with CASH
by Maisie and Poppy

AGE: **9 and 8**

WHERE: **New South Wales**

We get paid for doing our jobs with cash!

We divide it into Save, Splurge and Give. We use jam jars (decorated with crystals!) and a little purse for our Splurge money.

> **We get paid $8 a week, but only if we do our jobs!**

Mum and Dad get coins from the recycling station when we return our bottles and cans.

We love getting paid, it gets us really excited and makes us feel powerful.

If we are out, and we haven't brought our purse, we ask Mum if we can borrow the money. Sometimes she says yes, sometimes she says no.

We keep our jars next to our bunk beds.

My mum pays us with her BANK ACCOUNT

by Ada

AGE: **10**

WHERE: **New South Wales**

We get paid with an app!

My sister, Calla, and brother, Ellis, used to have coin jars with our names on them but Mum and Dad never had any coins, so we started using the Spriggy app.

> **I'm 10, and I get paid $10 a month allowance, with job money paid every week.**

I fill out a chart on the fridge when we do jobs, and then Dad works out how much we get paid. (We have to remind him, or we don't get paid!)

I like being able to see my money in Spriggy and decide how much I will leave in savings and how much I will move onto the card for spending. I really like having my own card for spending.

Our cards hang on the key rack so we don't lose them. If we want to buy something, we ask Mum or Dad to take us shopping.

Set up your money buckets!

Now for the fun stuff — it's time to decorate your money buckets!

Here's what you'll need:

Find any container you want — the weirder the better!

1 Three containers
Use whatever you have around the house as your three 'buckets': old jam jars, envelopes, plastic pockets and so on.

Your parents might have decided to pay you using a bank account, but you could still set up your **SPLURGE** bucket as a wallet.

2 Stickers!
Grab the stickers at the back of the book: the ones that say **SPLURGE**, **SAVE** and **GIVE**. You know what to do – stick them on your containers.

SPLURGE!

SAVE! **GIVE!**

3 Pens, pencils, coloured markers
Make those containers your own so that your little brother doesn't mistake your jars for his!

How to open your first bank account

When you get a bit older you'll graduate from using jam jars or envelopes to having your own bank account. A bank is a place where people store their money. The bank then gives you a plastic card to access your money, which you keep in your wallet or purse. You then pull it out and tap at the register in the shop to buy stuff.

The bank sometimes charges you a yearly fee for keeping and protecting your money, and they also reward you for saving by paying you some 'interest'. This is when they top up your savings with a little bit more money . . . just to keep you interest-ed!

Your parents will already have a bank account that they probably access via a card and an app on their phone.

Most banks only allow older kids to set up their own bank account, so it pays to do your research.

Here's what to look out for:

- **No bank fees**
  You don't want to be charged any fees from the bank. That means no account-keeping fees, and no ATM fees (for when you use an ATM to get your cash out).

- **Multiple savings accounts**
  You want the option to set up multiple savings accounts. In fact you need three, because these accounts become your money buckets. Name them **SPLURGE**, **SAVE** and **GIVE**.

MY TIP? The first thing you should do is google 'best Aussie bank accounts for students'.

On the next page, you'll meet a 14-year-old who set up her own bank account.

How I scored my very own bank account
by Ella

AGE: **14**

WHERE: **Victoria**

I'm 14 years old, so I kind of outgrew using jam jars. I wanted the independence of having an EFTPOS card. Plus, having a card made online shopping easier, and I didn't have to rely on using my parents' cards. So I decided to open my own bank account.

I ended up going with the bank my mum uses. Mum has been a customer of theirs for 30 years, and they are a community bank. So Mum and I went to the local branch to set it up. It was easy: **it only took 15 minutes**.

I love having my own bank account. It feels like I have more responsibility as it is a lot easier to access my own money, I can see my balance, and I can see my monthly review, which shows a summary of my purchases. It has taught me how to understand budgeting in real time and be accountable for what I spend.
It's exciting to see how quickly my money can grow when I don't spend it.
I'm now motivated to save for my first car!

Who gets to decide what jobs I do?

You get to suggest the jobs, your parents get to decide (they're the ones paying, after all!).

Do I really need three money buckets?

Yes, you do. It's the only way to make sure you have money set aside to get what you really want. This isn't just a cute idea for kids. I've taught my money bucket strategy to *millions* of adults, and every day someone, somewhere, tells me that it completely changed their life.

And it's going to work even better for you, because you don't have to spend years walking around with a hole in your bucket. You're learning the right way from the very start.

But I already do this using jam jars!

That's great! You're at the head of the class. Go eat some jam.

What about buying stuff online? How does that work?

That's up to your parents. The easiest option is to give them some money out of your SPLURGE bucket, and they'll buy it using their account.

Dude, I'm in high school, do you really expect me to carry jam jars into the school canteen?

When it comes to spending, most kids will use a wallet. Older kids like you should set up their own bank accounts like Ella.

Should my parents pay cash or via a bank account?

It's totally up to them. They're the ones who are paying. Both work. In fact there are some special accounts just for kids that they might want to check out. The most important thing is to make paying you as easy as possible.

It's time to get busy!

Next, go do your jobs really well . . . **all of them,**
plus your **Parent Pleasers**. You really want to impress
your parents with how good a job you can do.

Act like the
BOSS!

So you've done your jobs and you've set up your money buckets . . .

Now it's the moment you've been waiting for.

It's your new favourite day . . .

It's a good idea to make payday the same day and time every week.

(I suggest dinnertime, Sunday night . . . get your parents
to set a reminder in their phone).

Grab the PAID sticker from the back of the book and put it here:

But it's not all work and no play, next up you're in for a real treat.

It's time to
SPLURGE!

Now it's time for some FUN!

Phew, you've been busy!

You have earned yourself a treat.

But, just before you do, I want you to answer these three questions.

1 What is your SPLURGE bucket for?

....

....

2 What do you have to do to get the money
to put into your SPLURGE bucket?

....

....

3 Are you allowed to put all of your pay
into your SPLURGE bucket?

....

....

(Answers are at the bottom of the page, no peeking!)

So, how did you go?

Alright, now I am ordering you to **go out and SPLURGE!**

Chocolate? Lollies? Pokémon? A fart cushion? Pens? Something online?

As long as your parents approve, the choice is yours. You've worked hard.
You've earned it.

So enjoy your splurge!

ANSWERS: **1.** Splurging on little things you want. **2.** Work. **3.** No! The rule is that each bucket gets some money each payday.

YOU'RE ON FIRE!

What you've done in this step is pretty huge: by setting up your money buckets, you've instantly become better at managing your money than most adults!

Your parents must be absolutely beaming with pride.

HECK, I'm proud of you!

Go to the back of the book and get this sticker:

Stick it on the chart on page 22.

WELL DONE!

Now you might be looking at your brand spanking new money buckets and wondering how you can fill them as quickly as possible.

Well, that's exactly what I'm going to show you how to do.

The next step is the one that everyone goes **gaga** over:

You're about to become a **Barefoot Boss!**

STEP 3

Boss

BE A BAREFOOT BOSS

This step is the one that *everyone* gets excited about.

Here's the deal.

✓ You've set up your money buckets.

✓ You've started doing some jobs around the house and getting paid.

✓ Now you're raring to go, ready to fill up your money buckets as fast as you can.

And to do that you're going to do something really cool:

start **YOUR** very own business!

First up, you need an awesome business idea and I'm going to help you find one that you can make your very own.

Then I'll take you through my famous **SIX P PLAN**, which will show you how to set up your business in record time. We'll work out what you're going to do, how much to charge and who you can ask to help you out.

(Oh, and you'll also find out why my dad . . . hugs his car!)

Let's dig in!

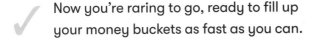

My first business idea

I was walking down the street when my very first business idea hit me like a gust of dust:

'I'm going to start a car washing business!'

I started counting the number of dirty cars I saw on my walk home. It was almost all of them.

My mind was buzzing. **If I charged $10 for a wash . . . I was totally going to clean up!**

So I burst through the door and excitedly pitched my brand-new business plan to my parents.

Dad seemed a little unsure. Folding his arms, he said, 'Scott, you've never actually washed a car before. How about I be your first customer, and then we'll see if you do a good enough job to charge real customers money.'

'YES!' I yelled, and immediately ran out to the carport.

See, my father loves his car. It's his pride and joy.
And I was about to make it sparkle!

On the way out I grabbed some dishwashing liquid for soap, a bucket and an old zip-up jumper to use as a washer.
Then I got to work.

Half an hour later I was done, and I called out to Dad to come and inspect it.

'That'll be $10!' I said, with my hand outstretched.

He looked at me. Then he looked at his car.

And then . . . he booted my washing bucket so hard it hurtled through the air and hit the back fence.

BANG!

'WHAT HAVE YOU DONE TO MY BEAUTIFUL CAR?'

he roared.

Uh-oh . . .

The zipper on the jumper had *scratched* the car!

The entire car looked like a four-year-old's kindergarten picture.
There were **scribbles everywhere**. Up and down the doors.
On the bonnet. **Even on the roof.**

Mum came out of the house scolding us both for making such a
racket . . . and then she saw the car and let out a high-pitched shriek.

I hid behind her.

I peered out and saw that Dad was hugging his car, and muttering
to himself.

My car washing business died that day.

Yet I did learn a valuable lesson:

SPLASH!

**It's great to have
an exciting idea,
but it pays to prepare
and think things through.**

It's time to meet the Barefoot Bosses . . .

These kids from all over Australia have sat where you are right now.

Yet they have created their very own businesses, and are now having

this is a 'dog-ear' just to be clear. I'm not talking about Betty ok!

the **EPIC** adventure of a lifetime.

You're about to meet:

- ⭐ the nine-year-old twins who are **turning their neighbours' trash into cash**

- ⭐ a kid who made **$3500 sitting in his room**

- ⭐ a 10-year-old girl who **gets paid to party**

- ⭐ a school kid who **gets paid $25 an hour to do homework**

- ⭐ the social media star who was **paid $10,000 for one post!**

And lots more . . .

What's really cool about these kids is that they not only share their business secrets with you . . .

YOU CAN BE INSPIRED BY THEIR IDEAS!

As you're reading through their stories, I want you to dog-ear the businesses you like. When you have read them all, you can come back and see which ones you might be able to do yourself.

Then we'll apply my step-by-step **SIX P PLAN** and you'll see that it's super simple to become a Barefoot Boss, like the kids you're about to meet.

We collect money that people throw away!

by Ryder and Alexis

OUR BUSINESS NAME:

The Collectors

AGE: **9**

WHERE: **Queensland**

We called our business 'The Collectors' because that's what we do: we collect our neighbours' bottles and cans and then we take them to a recycling centre and exchange them for money.

To grow our business we made up some flyers, letting people know we were a couple of kids who wanted to collect cans. We dropped them off around our neighbourhood. And it worked!

So far we have 28 customers. Most people are super friendly, but there was one grumpy guy who told us, 'Don't ever come around again!' We didn't let it get us down because most of our neighbours are really awesome, and getting to know them has been one of the best things about the job. Some of them make us laugh! Other customers live alone and we can tell they really enjoy our visits.

We spend about an hour collecting, half an hour at the tip, and about 10 minutes writing thank-you notes to our customers (which they love . . . one of our customers has kept the first letter we ever wrote to her stuck to the fridge!). Cans are the best to collect because you can crush them down, put them in a box, and hand them over to the people at the tip . . . and you still get 10 cents each!

At school I [Ryder] volunteer as an eco-marine – picking up litter, growing plants and stuff – so I love that our little business is helping the environment too. Mum and Dad are really proud of what we're doing, and we're really proud of ourselves.

We are saving up for an epic overseas holiday to visit our grandparents who live in the United Kingdom. We haven't seen them for ages. Oh, we also saved up for a puppy, too.

How much money do you earn?

So far we've made **$721** in a few months! I've earned more doing recycling than my entire life savings (money from relatives at birthdays and doing jobs around the house).

How hard is this for other kids to do? (easy? hard-ish? tough?)

It's pretty easy. You just need to be friendly and chatty (and buy a $40 trolley from Bunnings).

Easy

> **I love that our little business is helping the environment too.**

DID YOU KNOW?

Most recycling stations in Australia will pay you 10 cents for every container you deliver. I know, 10 cents a pop for something most people throw away! You'll never look at your neighbour's bin the same way again!

Before you start collecting drink containers, do a google and make sure a container deposit scheme (CDS) is available in your area.

I set up my own online shop!
by Charlotte

MY BUSINESS NAME:

Bold Pineapple

AGE: 12

WHERE: Victoria

My shop is called 'Bold Pineapple' because being a pineapple means to 'stand tall, wear a crown and be sweet on the inside'.

I create and sell homemade earrings and lip gloss packs. They're not that hard to make. First, I buy all my supplies either from Amazon or the local art store. It takes me around two hours to make my earrings, and I sell them for $4 (or $5 if they're custom-made). Making lip glosses is quicker — I can make 12 in an hour. I sell them for $10 per lip gloss pack, and I make around $3 per pack after paying for all my expenses.

I love making my products and promoting them (sometimes I even put pictures up on social media on the way to a netball game!). However, in the beginning I had no idea how to set up an online store.

I set up my website with GoDaddy, and it costs around $300 a year. GoDaddy makes setting up a website really simple. They have templates you can copy to set up an online store really fast.

The next problem was that I didn't really know how much I should charge, or how to handle postage, so I reached out to a family friend

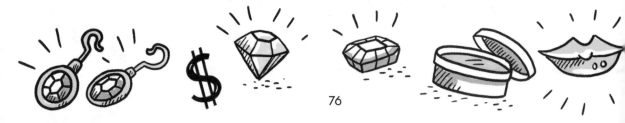

who had an online business and asked for their help. They were great. After they helped set it up it was pretty easy; you just print postage stickers from the Australia Post website.

When you're starting a business, you don't have to do it all on your own. You should always ask for help. My dad says he's really enjoyed helping me with it, and we've both learnt so much. Dad loves telling people about my store too!

How much money do you earn?

Since I started a year ago, I've made **$1500** in sales . . . but after I paid back my dad for the set-up costs (paying for the website, buying supplies) I've kept around $250. Being a vegetarian, animals are really important to me, so I donate to the RSPCA with every product sold.

How hard is this for other kids to do? (easy? hard-ish? tough?)

Tough! It can be difficult to set up, which is why you should get help from your parents or an expert who has their own store. But once you are up and running it's pretty easy. I'm not sure how long I'll have the shop for, but it's been a great experience.

> **When you're starting a business, you don't have to do it all on your own. You should always ask for help.**

Tough

DID YOU KNOW?

Setting up a shop in a shopping centre can cost over $100,000 dollars. However, you can set up an online store for a couple of hundred dollars or start an Etsy shop for free! And even better, you can sell your stuff to people all over the world.

My $10,000 dog!
by Ashleigh

MY BUSINESS NAME:

Ashleigh's Dog Walking and Sitting

AGE: **12**

WHERE: **Victoria**

I love dogs, so one day I made up some signs and flyers that said 'Dog sitting for $5' and I put them up at the local dog park and did a mailbox drop. But I didn't get one single response!

Now I use a pet-sitting app called Mad Paws to find my customers. There are heaps of other sites as well, just google to see what's available in your area. I still wanted to charge $5, but Dad told me that I shouldn't set my price too cheap. So I decided to charge $35 per night and I got a great response. Actually, I was too busy so I increased my price to $49 a night.

My fee includes: the dog being walked once or twice a day, food (plus treats!), sometimes a wash (if they sit in poop), and LOTS and LOTS of playtime with me! All up it takes me around an hour-and-a-half.

First someone will message me about dog-sitting via the app. Mum gets the notifications on her phone. Then we

THAT'S A PAW-SOME BUSINESS!

host a meet-and-greet with the owner and the dog in our home, and let them know I am responsible for feeding, walking, entertaining and cleaning up. There are a lot of dog-sitters out there, so the hardest part at the start is trying to stand out. I send the owner lots of photos of their dogs, which makes them happy and gets me good reviews!

My dream is to become a vet when I'm older, so this is such an awesome business for me.

How much money do you earn?

I'm in my first year of the business and have so far made **$10,000!**

How hard is this for other kids to do? (easy? hard-ish? tough?)

Hard-ish. When I told my best friend what I was doing she loved it and wanted to know all about the dogs and would come over and play with them. I think she wishes she could dog-sit too, but it's not for everyone. You have to make sure it suits your family and any pets you have yourself, and that you have the right house and backyard.

hard-ish

> **The hardest part at the start is trying to stand out from other businesses like yours.**

DID YOU KNOW?

There are actually more pets in Australia than people! Yes, that's right. There are 30 million pets but only 26 million people. And dogs are our most popular pets, with over five million pooches across the nation.

That's a lot of dogs to walk every day!

My nonna's secret recipe!
by Violetta

MY BUSINESS NAME:

Gnocchi di Violetta

AGE: **14**

WHERE: **Victoria**

During the COVID lockdown in 2021, I was getting a bit down so Mum and Dad told me to take a break from online school classes and do something that brought me joy. I thought, 'Cooking makes me happy', so I dusted off my Italian nonna's recipes and got going.

My parents said my gnocchi was so tasty that I started to think I could sell it to people in our street. So we texted a few of our neighbours and within the first two weeks I'd made 12 kilos of homemade gnocchi with a Tuscan pomarola tomato sauce . . . and I'd sold the lot!

These days I spend around five hours a week cooking, mainly on weekends and after school. Mostly I just put some music on, zone out and get to work. Sometimes Dad Zooms my nonna in Italy while I'm cooking and she calls out, 'Brava Violetta!' which means 'very good!'

Our family friend Tess helped me design my website. We also use a great online ordering platform called Big Cartel which allows you to load up to five products for free. People can order, choose which day for delivery, and choose whether they want to pick up or have it

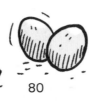

delivered. I keep it simple: all I sell is gnocchi and sauce for $25. The ingredients cost around $8, so I make $17 per sale, and I charge $5 extra for delivery if it's close to my home.

At the start I had to learn from my mistakes. I had a customer who wasn't happy because the gnocchi they received was squashed. I was a bit stressed about it, but I immediately made another batch and delivered it to them personally to apologise.

Making my gnocchi and getting out to deliver it and say hi to lots of people has really helped me gain confidence.

How much money do you earn?

I started the business in September 2021 and made **$2000** in the first eight months. The business paid for itself really quickly! I love how I can make money doing something I love.

How hard is this for other kids to do? (easy? hard-ish? tough?)

hard-ish

Cooking is easy, but making it into a business is hard-ish, so make sure it's something you enjoy doing!

> 6 **At the start I had to learn from my mistakes . . . now I love how I can make money doing something I love.** 9

DID YOU KNOW?

The average Aussie household spends $92.08 a week on eating out and takeaway, according to Budget Direct. That's a lot of Happy Meals! This explains why local businesses that make delicious, nutritious food are absolutely thriving right now!

I made $3500 from my room!
by Liam

AGE: **14**

WHERE: **New South Wales**

I love mountain biking and having the latest stuff. My parents said that if I wanted more gear I'd have to buy it myself but it was taking too long to save for anything good just doing my jobs at home. One day I noticed some of Mum's old household decorations.

With Mum's permission, I ended up listing them on Facebook Marketplace and getting $300 for them! I was so excited because I had done it all myself — taking the photos, writing the description, posting it online, answering the enquiries and arranging to meet up with the customer.

When I started I didn't have strong negotiation skills. I wasn't sure about the kinds of questions buyers might ask me, and I wondered if I would be taken seriously. I bought some small items from Facebook Marketplace so I got a feel for how others negotiate.

I learnt that sometimes people start their prices too low. Instead, start high. I might list something at $400 when I would be happy to get $200. Usually I get a higher amount than I expect. It's also good to research what people might be willing to pay for similar items.

I'm also pretty particular with the images — I take time to ensure they look good by putting the items in front of a white wall or with nice backgrounds. I use my phone to take the images.

I generally have one or two items for sale at a time. It probably takes about two hours of my time a week. I'm really proud of myself because I have become more independent.

How much money do you earn?

I've made over **$3500**, which has paid for my mountain bike and (second-hand) tech equipment.

How hard is this for other kids to do? (easy? hard-ish? tough?)

It can be tough! You need to be pretty good at talking and being social with people because you get a lot of messages and questions about the items you're selling. Also, your parents need to be on board. After all, you're dealing with strangers.

Tough

The easiest things to sell are clothes and electronics (I recently bought a pair of Beats headphones for $50, relisted them, and sold them for $180!).

> **Even if you're a bit younger and don't have a lot of experience, you can find ways to get what you want.**

DID YOU KNOW?

The average family has a whopping $5400 worth of trash lying around inside their homes! That's according to online marketplace Gumtree, and they should know!

Old toys, sporting equipment, musical instruments, books and clothes are shoved in cupboards just gathering dust. Gather them up and turn them into treasure!

I have a bumper lawn mowing business!

by Paxton

MY BUSINESS NAME:

Pax's Handyman Services

AGE: 10

WHERE: Queensland

I started by mowing our neighbour's lawn. It was fun. However, when Dad asked whether I wanted to get more customers, I told him I was really nervous approaching grown-ups and pitching my services.

So I decided to create my own work shirts that say 'Pax's Handyman Services'. It didn't cost much and it really helps with my confidence that I look the part and have a uniform. (I've also designed a collared business shirt for when I'm doing business.)

On average I do five lawns a week, mostly after school or on weekends. Each lawn takes me about an hour to do. Customers pay anywhere between $25 and $50 a lawn. Sometimes people give tips too!

I have a spreadsheet that lists dates, jobs, customers, and how much they paid. I don't have many outgoings. I've spent $60 on fuel since I started.

My customers loved my work shirt so much that I decided to design bumper stickers using PicCollage and I give them away to my clients.

It was fun to come up with the picture and names, and there are now plenty of cars rolling down the street with a 'Pax's Handyman Services' sticker on the back of their car. It's great advertising!

The best moment is when I finish a job (I check everything twice) and my customer comes out and gives me a fist bump and tells me I've done a great job. That makes me feel really proud.

How much money do you earn?

I'm always a bit nervous giving people a price, so I just say, 'Pay me whatever you think is reasonable.' And guess what? They always end up paying more than I would have asked for! So far I've made **$1500** in six months!

How hard is this for other kids to do? (easy? hard-ish? tough?)

It's easy. Play less video games and do more mowing!

❛ I created my own bumper stickers to advertise my business! ❜

Easy

DID YOU KNOW?

Looking the part and wearing a name tag are the easiest and fastest ways to boost your confidence *and* make customers friendlier towards you.

Why?

Wearing a name tag means your customers feel welcome and they instantly can see you know what you're doing.

Don't have a name tag? Yes you do, it's in the back of the book.

My bow-WOW biscuit business!
by Ryder

MY BUSINESS NAME:

DOG SHOP
Homemade Pet Bribes & Treats by Ryder

AGE: 6

WHERE: Queensland

We'd just finished baking some biscuits for ourselves and I said to Mum, 'Why don't we bake some for our dogs too?'

So we researched recipes online – there are heaps! We made a batch and our dogs loved them! Then we decided to put my dog biscuits on our school Facebook page to see if there was any interest in people buying some. We got 70 orders from school, family and friends!

Now we do a cook-up once a fortnight and that lasts us two weeks. Mum does all the baking (I help cut out the shapes) and I am in charge of selling and marketing the biscuits. We sell them at our local markets two weekends a month, and also through a local pet food shop, so we have to make sure they have stock. We use social media to promote the business. Customers send us photos and videos of their dogs eating the biscuits, which we upload to Instagram and Facebook.

Our biscuits are fresh, and we have so many different flavours: peanut butter, pumpkin, banana, berry, sweet potato and bacon. We charge 40 cents for treats and bribes, and 80 cents for fancies, which are bigger treats. We also sell the treats in bags: $5 for a small bag (17 treats),

$10 for a medium bag (30 treats) and $20 for a large bag (55 treats).

The large bag of treats costs us $8 in ingredients so we make $12. We cut the costs — but not the quality — where we can. For example, we get free eggs from neighbours in return for our scraps for their chooks, and we often get pumpkins in exchange for treats.

It has really helped me get better at maths and talking to adults. My parents are really proud of me and so are my teachers. When I get older I might work at Kmart — maybe be the boss!

How much money do you earn?

I have approximately **$600** in the bank, even after I have donated lots of money to our local dog shelter. And my first purchase was a PAW Patrol watch!

How hard is this for other kids to do? (easy? hard-ish? tough?)

It's hard-ish. It's pretty easy to make dog treats if you have help from your parents. Selling them takes effort, though, especially at the local markets. You have to be brave.

hard-ish

> **The business has really helped me get better at maths and talking to adults.**

DID YOU KNOW?

Around half of all dog owners allow their four-legged friend to share their bed. Dogs dream like people. Yawning is contagious — even for dogs. But do you know what the most interesting fact is?

The average dog owner spends $1627 per dog each year, according to the RSPCA.

YUM!

My slimy business!
by Hannika

MY BUSINESS NAME:

Slime Mountain

AGE: **12**

WHERE: **Victoria**

I started making my own slime when I was 10. There are heaps of recipes online, and it was really fun, so I began teaching kids in my neighbourhood how to make it. I knew that I wanted to start my own business, so I nagged Mum and Dad and eventually they said yes.

Before I started, I did loads of research. I went to different shops, did a webinar with a famous American 'slimer' and learnt heaps. I even ordered a competitor's slime to see what packaging they used. Mum and Dad loaned me the money to buy all the ingredients, on the condition that I paid them back before I kept any money.

I started selling slime at markets to see what was popular. I work a full day each week on Slime Mountain. Mum and my sister Michaela help with orders and packaging, and I make big batches of slime, which takes about two hours.

I sell my slime for between $9 and $13. Around half the price is the cost of the ingredients. It took 6 months to pay back my parents, so now I get to keep the other half.

I launched my Etsy shop around Christmas time and I got heaps of orders. I offered free postage to locals who ordered through

Etsy, and I asked them to leave a review to improve my Etsy rating. So far I've made over a thousand sales!

My parents are really proud of me — they tell me all the time! 'Don't give up' is what I've learnt, be persistent. Even when you are told no, keep going. I just kept asking Mum and Dad until finally they agreed, and as a family we have made this business a success.

How much money do you earn?

I've earned about **$6000** in 18 months. I didn't expect it to take off as much as it did!

How hard is this for other kids to do? (easy? hard-ish? tough?)

Hard-ish. If you want to start a business and you're passionate about it, then you should go for it. It's exciting to get orders, but there are some boring bits like packing all the orders, so you have to love it. For me, I feel like I can do things that I couldn't before. I feel like a real entrepreneur.

hard-ish

> **'This is what I've learnt: don't give up. Be persistent.**

DID YOU KNOW?

You have slime on you right now!

It's true. The natural version of slime is called mucus, which is just a fancy scientific name for . . . SNOT!

Slime (the toy, not the snot) was invented by Mattel Toys almost 50 years ago. They wanted to make it as gross and snot-like as possible, so they created oozy, sticky, green goo and put it in a toy trash can. It was an instant hit!

I get paid to do homework!
by Matilda

MY BUSINESS NAME:

The Maths Mate

AGE: **13**

WHERE: **Queensland**

I have a passion for teaching so I decided to start my own tutoring business, helping out primary school kids with their maths homework.

To find customers, I designed an advertisement using PicCollage, and Mum and Dad posted to Facebook to see if any parents wanted to hire me to tutor their kids.

I felt super nervous about the first lesson. My eight-year-old client was hiding from me and it was a bit awkward. I had to figure out how I was going to teach him, what his level of ability was, and the best approach to take.

One way I learnt to overcome my nerves was to be prepared. I made sure that next time, I had a list of 12 different activities we could do. Preparation gives me options if something isn't working.

(And now that eight-year-old student loves me!)

I help younger kids in my school community. I do two one-hour sessions a week, helping a student in Grade 3 and one in Grade 6. I charge their parents $25 an hour. My students' parents are

5×8
$= 40$

really grateful that I am providing a service that they can't deliver themselves. A lot of them struggle to get kids to do their homework, let alone trying to teach them fractions! I'm the fun one who can come along and teach them through games and keep them engaged.

I get such a sense of accomplishment when my students get it, when they learn something new. I ride home feeling happy! My sessions are fun. The fact that it counts as work experience is an added bonus. When I grow up I want to be a maths professor. Even now as a 13-year-old it's pretty cool to say to my friends, 'I'm off to work!'

How much money do you earn?

I've earned around **$600** in the last year.

$$6 \times 9 \qquad \frac{1}{3} \times \frac{2}{5}$$

How hard is this for other kids to do? (easy? hard-ish? tough?)

Tough! But just remember you don't have to be the best at a particular subject. Just think, 'I'm prepared for this, I know fractions and I can do it' or whatever the subject you love is. Once it's set up and you get some experience, it becomes easier. And you become more confident — and confidence builds confidence! It's great that I can set my own hours and I get paid more than working at Macca's. If you have an idea, give it go! What's the worst that could happen?

Tough

> **I have become more confident — and confidence builds confidence!**

DID YOU KNOW?

One in seven school kids has a tutor!

Think about it: you could turn your gold stars into gold coins and actually get paid to share your knowledge and help out a younger student! Tutors earn anywhere from $15 to over $80 an hour!

I get paid to draw!
by Scarlett

MY BUSINESS NAME:

Cards by the Print

AGE: 8

WHERE: Victoria

I set up my own card shop when I was six and began selling them at the end of our driveway. However, business was slow (and I got wet when it rained!) so I spoke to our local cafe to see if they would allow me to sell my handmade cards. They said yes!

I design cards for about half an hour before school each morning. I use card paper that I get from a craft store that also has matching envelopes. I use textas, crayons and pencils, and sometimes my grandparents give me stickers to use. Recently I got some wooden letters and glued the words 'Hello Beautiful' on a card. I like to do themed cards for things like Mother's Day.

I deliver my cards twice a week and collect the money from sales at the cafe. We have an honesty box. I like speaking with the cafe owner about what the customers like and say about my cards, so I know what designs are selling well. I sell them for $2 each and the materials cost 20 cents, so I make $1.80 per card.

When I'm not creating cards, I spend my time looking at the property market. I'm saving to buy my first property, and I plan to rent it out until I'm an adult. That's my long-term goal, but my card shop also helps me with short-term goals too, like treating my friends with icy poles.

How much money do you earn?

So far I have made **$140**.

How hard is this for other kids to do? (easy? hard-ish? tough?)

Easy, and it's really fun. Just start making cards. Do an hour each day to start with and get the details right. Just try your best and you can make it work.

> Easy

> **Do an hour each day to start with and get the details right. Just try your best and you can make it work.**

DID YOU KNOW?

Did you know that the average Aussie gets 22 birthday, Christmas, and 'Sorry my dog pooped on your couch' cards every year?

Aussies spend a mind-boggling $500 million on cards every year . . . and we're the third-largest purchasers of cards in the world.

Yet here's the thing: most cards are a bit cheesy, and they can cost as much as $10! You could make way cooler cards, right?

I get paid to party!
by Sophie

MY BUSINESS NAME:

Glitter and Glam

AGE: **10**

WHERE: **ACT**

I got the idea for my business when I organised my brother's birthday party. A few parents noticed I was doing a good job and asked me whether I'd plan their kids' parties.

To prepare, I researched the most popular party ideas, worked out what games and activities I could do and practised doing them. I then created a list of all the party supplies I'd need. Right now, the main parties I do are 'glitter and glam' and I also do 'glitter and tattoos' (fake ones, not real!). Gecko tattoos are the most popular, though my favourites are the mythical ones like mermaids — so I can use multiple colours like red for their hair. It takes two to five minutes per tattoo.

When I have a booking for a party, it takes about an hour to get ready and I do that the week before. I arrive at the party 15 minutes early to set up my table with the tattoos and flyers and make it look nice. And then the average party goes for two hours, so all up around 3.5 hours per party.

I get my party supplies (glitter, glue and tattoos) from Face Paint Shop Australia, and it costs around $15 per party. I charge $30 per hour per party and I split the money with Mum, who pays for the supplies. I don't have a website or Instagram but I have created flyers (using Canva and PicCollage) that I hand out to parents at the parties to get new business.

At my very first party it was pretty cute because all the little kids wanted to help me, then one of them kicked over the glitter, but it was okay — I had extra supplies. It was a success. All the parents said I did an awesome job.

How much money do you earn?

So far I've done about 10 parties in total so I've earned about **$300**.

How hard is this for other kids to do? (easy? hard-ish? tough?)

Hard-ish. Don't worry if you're not getting customers to start with. Hand out flyers, and advertise with posters at your local shops. If you put in a bit of blood, sweat and tears, you'll succeed!

> **Don't worry if you're not getting customers to start with. If you put in a bit of blood, sweat and tears, you'll succeed!**

hard-ish

DID YOU KNOW?

Kids' birthdays are big business! The average parent spends a whopping $270 on their kid's birthday party . . . and that doesn't even include the birthday present. (That's extra!)

And given the average kid goes to eight birthday parties a year . . . that's a lot of lolly bags!

I'm a TikTok star!
by <u>Tommy</u>

AGE: **16**

WHERE: **Victoria**

I was 14 when I started and Mum didn't really like me being on social media. She was worried I was just wasting time. So I explained that I was actually spending my time creating content, rather than just staring at the screen.

I didn't set out to become a social media star. I was just playing around making videos that I thought were cool (and a bit dark). I didn't know whether people would like what I was doing, but I didn't really care because I loved doing it.

I spend a lot of time and effort making my TikTok videos – I do things like uncover spooky past events – but it doesn't feel like work. It's fun. I've gained 7.6 million followers in a little over a year. When I started on YouTube I built over 200,000 subscribers in the first three months.

People think that building a following should be easy, just because they're on social media and have a phone. It's not easy. You have to work really hard at coming up with cool ideas, and even then it will probably take a while to break through.

I was paid $10,000 for my first promotion. Mum nearly fainted!

How much money do you earn?

I have made **$13,000** (so far). It sounds amazing (and it is), but I don't count on it. I also work two other jobs in our small town just in case it doesn't work out!

How hard is this for other kids to do? (easy? hard-ish? tough?)

It's very, very, VERY tough.

Don't do it for the money. Don't do it to get followers. Put your time into creating content you love. If it works — and it's a long shot — you'll be happy. And if you're doing what you love, don't give up. Don't worry about what your friends think. If they're not supportive then they're probably jealous. Be yourself. Work hard.

> **Put your time into creating content you love. If it works — and it's a long shot — you'll be happy.**

Tough

WARNING: Tommy's content isn't appropriate for little kids.

DID YOU KNOW?

A study in the United States found that almost 9 in 10 kids want to become a social media star.

And it makes perfect sense. After all, who wouldn't want to get paid to hang out at home and make videos?

My flower power!
by Ava

MY BUSINESS NAME:

Ava's Flowers

AGE: 7

WHERE: South Australia

Nana and I came up with a very cool business idea. We could cut flowers from some old protea bushes on our farm and put them at the end of the road at a stall with an honesty box for people to pay. Proteas are popular!

I made a sign from an old blackboard: 'Ava's Flowers, $5 per bunch' and put out five bunches on the first day. Mum put a photo on Instagram to announce we were open for business.

Dad was worried that no-one would buy my flowers because we live on a very quiet country road. He said, 'Don't be too disappointed if you don't sell any flowers, love. It's great just to have a go.'

I was so excited to get off the school bus that afternoon and check my honesty box. There was $25 waiting for me. I'd completely sold out!

At the start the hardest thing for me was having to wait for the adults to cut the proteas for me, because I didn't have my own secateurs – they're like strong scissors for cutting stems of plants. But I got my very own pink secateurs, so now I can cut my own. It takes me around six hours each week to prepare everything, and check the flowers at the end of the driveway every morning and night.

My parents are definitely proud of me. I've learnt that you have to work hard on your business to get the prize. Some businesses sell proteas for $5 a stem but I wanted to keep mine at $1 dollar a stem so that people could afford them. If they can't, there will be less customers and less happy people.

It's so exciting to check my sales when I get off the school bus each day. In two years, no-one has been dishonest! We sell out most days at $5 a bunch. I like making people happy with my flowers and I'm really proud that I get to brighten people's day. I love taking orders . . . people stop me in the supermarket, after school, all around town.

How much money do you earn?

I made **$700** in eight weeks! I'm investing part of it in the share market.

How hard is this for other kids to do? (easy? hard-ish? tough?)

Easy, if you already have the flowers growing. You don't even need a busy street to sell your flowers!

Easy

> ❝ **It's such a thrill to check my sales when I get off the school bus each day.** ❞

DID YOU KNOW?

Flower power comes in many shapes and sizes! Broccoli isn't a vegetable . . . it's actually a flower!?

Yet that doesn't mean you should buy your mum a bunch of broccoli for Mother's Day. In fact, Aussies spend $200 million buying flowers for their mums, just on that one day! Now that smells like a HUGE business opportunity!

My suitcase rummage!
by Hannah

AGE: **9**

WHERE: **Queensland**

We'd been doing the jam jars at home for a while but I wanted a quick way to make more money to add to my jars. I wanted to have a stall to sell things.

Mum suggested we go to a suitcase rummage. It's like a market, but instead of setting up tables people sell stuff out of a suitcase. My mum registered us for a rummage in the city, which cost $33. She said I could bring three suitcases to sell from.

I spent ages collecting stuff around the house that we didn't use any more, like old toys and clothes that didn't fit me. My brother also gave me some big Ninja Turtles to sell for $50. I made sure I collected enough stuff to fill those three suitcases!

On the day of the rummage, Mum and Nanny and I went into the city and set out our suitcases. It was so much fun! There were lots of shoppers looking through my suitcases. Some tried to get me to discount my prices. Most people were really friendly and I enjoyed chatting to them. I was in charge of writing down all my sales and giving people the correct change (we had been to the bank so we had lots of coins). It was a really long day, but we came home with almost empty suitcases!

How much money do you earn?

I made **$350** in sales for the day. I even paid Mum back for the cost of the site, gave my brother the money we got for selling the Ninja Turtles, and bought some handmade soap for Nanny for coming along and supporting me. The rest went into my jars!

How hard is this for other kids to do? (easy? hard-ish? tough?)

Easy – if you are confident. But for people like me who are a bit shy, you'll have fun too – you will get more confident as the day goes on!

Easy

> **For people like me who are a bit shy, you'll have fun too – you will get more confident as the day goes on!**

DID YOU KNOW?

Most capital cities hold mini markets – like suitcase rummages – a few times a year (google it!). Otherwise, do one in your street. There are only three steps:

1. Grab a suitcase.
2. Go round the house and throw stuff in that you want to sell – as long as your parents say okay!
3. Open your suitcase and start selling . . . and count your money!

You're probably thinking . . .

I don't think my parents will let me start a business.

I think they will *definitely* let you. In fact, let me tell you why:

Because you're going to learn loads of stuff.

And because they'll be insanely proud of you!

I don't have time.

You can start off doing something quick and easy, like selling stuff around your house or doing a suitcase rummage. But it's really important to let your parents know that you'll wait until *they* have time to help — they are very busy too!

I don't have any money to set up my shop, or pay for ingredients.

Many Barefoot Bosses kick-started their business by getting a small loan from their parents or grandparents. They paid it back when they made some sales. You could even draw up an agreement and sign it! Or use your SAVE bucket for kick-starter funds.

I don't know anything about tax.

Actually, you're probably not thinking that, because you don't know what tax is, right? Well, tax is sharing a little of what you earn with the government to help run the country (think roads, schools and hospitals). Talk to your parents and get them to look up the ATO website. Search for 'income if you're under 18'.

I'm scared of talking to customers.

I totally understand, and this is one of the biggest benefits of becoming a Barefoot Boss: you're going to become very brave! Just remember S.E.A. (Smile, Eye Contact, Ask Questions) and you'll be amazed at how quickly your confidence grows.

What if your business doesn't work out?

It might . . . and that's not only totally okay,

it's totally normal!

My first business idea (remember the car washing) was a disaster!

Just ask my Dad.

Yet I didn't quit. I just shook it off and tried something else . . . can you imagine if I'd chucked a tanty and given up? You wouldn't be reading this book right now!

There are two reasons why **you should not be scared of failure**.

First, dreaming up the idea and planning it all is what everyone agrees is *the* most exciting part!

Second, you have a head start on other kids. You can be inspired by the business ideas of the **Barefoot Bosses** in this book. Learn from them. Their ideas have all been road-tested, and they work really well.

Even better, in a moment I'll take you through my **SIX P PLAN,** which will show you how to take any of the ideas you've chosen and make them a success.

Instawoof

B Instagram isn't just for cute dogs! Get your parents to take photos of you working in your business.

Remember those pages you dog-eared?

I want you to go back and look at the businesses you chose and to reread the section called 'How hard is this for other kids to do?'

My tips?

First, think about starting with something the Barefoot Bosses say is easy. (Remember, you can always move on to the hard-ish and tough businesses as your confidence grows.)

Second, and this is really important:

make sure you're doing something you love . . . because you're going to be doing a lot of it!

If you haven't dog-eared anything, don't worry . . . I'll help you brainstorm a few options.

Soon you'll be buzzing with your own business idea, and dying to bring it to life!

LIKE A BOSS!

Your business ideas

What do you love doing?

....

....

....

Which Barefoot Boss businesses do you like?

....

....

....

You're going to be making stuff or doing stuff for money.
Are you a maker or a doer?

....

What could you **make** to sell?

....

....

....

What could you **do** for other people?

....

....

....

Ask for help!

Next up is the *really* important part: find people who can help you get started.

The more advice you ask for and the more research you do, the easier and quicker you can turn your idea into reality.

Everyone needs help when they start out.

(Plus, most people are going to be totally stoked that *you* asked *them* for help).

First, think of all the things you'll need help with. Start with these and make your own list:

* setting up a website or online shop

* ordering supplies

* finding customers

* packaging and postage

* getting to places.

Now think about people you know who have the skills or experience and time to help you.

Perhaps a friend of your parents already has an online shop (see Charlotte's story on page 76). Or perhaps your family can help with packing orders (see Hannika's story on page 88).

Find experts and watch their YouTube videos. Ryder and his mum found a dog biscuit recipe online (see page 86). Liam learnt how to write good ads for Facebook Marketplace by looking at how other people did it (see page 82). Violetta used her grandmother's tried-and-true recipe to make gnocchi to sell (see page 80).

THE SIX P PLAN

My step-by-step **SIX P PLAN** means it is super simple to become a Barefoot Boss. All you need to do is answer six questions and out will pop your very own business plan. Let's go through the questions one by one.

1 PARENTS:
Have your parents given their approval?

It's really important to get your parents' permission before you start your business. You're probably going to need their help, and maybe even a loan from them, so it pays to ask their permission first.

2 PEOPLE:
Who can help you get started?

Starting a business can feel really overwhelming. But you don't need to do it on your own. You've made a list of all the people who can help you (parents, family friends and other experts), so ask them for help!

3 PRODUCT:
What are you going to sell?

This is pretty simple. Depending on the business you've chosen, you're either going to be a 'maker' (making stuff) or a 'doer' (doing stuff). So if you're mowing lawns you're selling lawn mowing services. If you're selling slime, it's boogers!

4 PRICE:
How much are you going to sell it for?

Most kids sell their stuff or their services way too cheap. Remember Ashleigh the dog-walker back on page 78? She set her dog-sitting price at $5 and didn't get a single response. Then she put her price up to $35, and then $49 a night, and she was run off her paws with customers! So have a go at setting your own price, but show it to your chosen experts. They'll be able to tell you whether it's the right price.

5 PROMOTION:
How are you going to get the word out?

Will you get your parents to do a social media post? Perhaps create a flyer and do a letterbox drop in your neighborhood? Or maybe you'll make some posters? In fact, I've got a little present for you at the end of the book (don't look yet!) that explains to your customers what your business is about.

6 PLACE:
Where are you going to do it?

This one is pretty simple. If you are a maker, are you going to set up a stand in your driveway, sell at a local market or open an online shop? If you're a doer, will your service be local or online?

FINAL TIP: Go back and reread your favourite Barefoot Boss story, and look for *their* answers to the SIX Ps.

Your SIX P PLAN

Your Barefoot Boss business name:

....

What your business does:

....

....

Your six Ps

PARENTS: have your parents given their approval?

yes ◯ no ◯

PEOPLE: who can help you get started?

....

PRODUCT: what are you going to sell?

....

PRICE: how much are you going to sell it for?
(Hint: most kids start too cheap.)

....

PROMOTION: how are you going to get the word out?

....

PLACE: where are you going to do it?

....

CONGRATULATIONS!
You're
THE BOSS!

If I was standing next to you, I'd give you a fist bump.

By getting to Step 3, you're way way ahead of most other kids your age.

Go to the back of the book and get this sticker:

Stick it on the chart on page 22.

Well done!

And you're now on your way to starting your very own business. Do you know how impressive that is?

It's **VERY IMPRESSIVE.**

Most businesses only hire older kids. Fast food joints like McDonald's and KFC will only hire you once you're 14. And supermarkets like Woolies and Coles will make you wait another year . . . till you turn 15.

Let me tell you a little secret: most teenagers who apply for their first part-time job feel really nervous, because they have **ZERO** experience.

Not you. You're brave. You're organised. You're confident and you know how to talk to people. You are the boss of your **OWN BUSINESS!**

You'll have Ronald McDonald in a McFlurry to hire you, because you'll be the one kid with oodles of experience!

Your money buckets are soon going to be overflowing, which is why Step 4 is all about how to get what you **REALLY** want!

STEP 4

GET
WHAT YOU
WANT

On your marks . . .

This is the step where **all your hard work pays off**, and you get what you want!

WOO HOO!

First, you're going to dream up one big goal . . . something you *really* want:

A bike? A boat? A puppy?

Whatever you decide on (and I've got loads of ideas to help you decide), I'll show you how you can turbocharge your savings and reach your goal quicker than you ever thought possible!

Plus, I'll show you how I shop for things and get huge discounts and you're going to go on a super-fun treasure hunt.

This is going to be a **BLAST!**

Along the way we'll meet:

★ two brothers who hunted down a cheap Nintendo Switch

★ the little girl who saved up and bought her dream house

★ a six-year-old who paid for his family to go on a desert adventure

★ a real-life dinosaur hunter

★ the twins who found a second-hand friend.

Oh, and a mega-successful social media influencer will share his *big secret* with you.

How to make all your Christmases come at once

Nothing beats the feeling of waking up on Christmas morning.

It's still dark outside. It's dead quiet. Everyone else is fast asleep.

And then you remember . . .

It's CHRISTMAS MORNING!

So you sprint into the lounge room and catch your first glimpse of what Santa has left under the tree.

For me, that's when my heart starts beating fast, and all I can think of is one thing:

Did I get what I really wanted?

Because there's always **ONE PRESENT** you want more everything else, right?

So I'm about to show you how you can get what you *really* want on your own . . .

much, much cheaper than you can find it at the shops . . .

and you won't have to wait till Christmas rolls around again!

The social media influencer's **BIG SECRET**

Tommy is a Barefoot Boss (we met him on page 96).

He's TikTok famous, with 7.6 million followers lapping up his content.

With a few taps on his phone, he got paid $10,000 . . .

for **ONE POST!**

Can you imagine being able to do that?

Tommy spends his time creating awesome content for his fans . . .
and he can earn more per hour than most adults who have been to uni,
wear a suit to work, sit in boring meetings and spend their time at work
replying to pointless emails and stuff.

Tommy is **KILLING it!**

Yet it gets even better.

He does it all on a second-hand iPhone.

> ' **They were trying to sell
> the phone for $600 . . .
> but I bargained them down to
> $500. I create all my stuff with it.
> You don't need the latest gear.** '
>
> Tommy

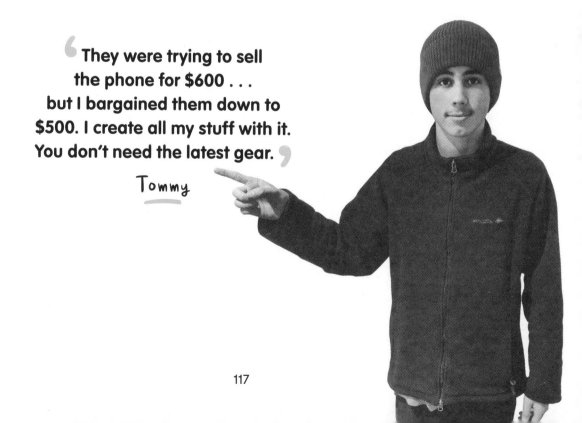

We've all been brainwashed to think 'expensive = better'

And do you know why?

Because that's how businesses make their money.

So instead of this, I say:

GOOD AS NEW IS BETTER THAN NEW

Why?

Because you can buy the exact same thing for practically nothing after someone else has done the unwrapping for you. It's second-hand, still good as new, and it's now **dirt cheap**.

You rarely hear the message that good is better than new. That's because all around the world companies spend about $1 trillion dollars **each year** on marketing and ads (and social media influencers!) that try to convince you to buy their brand new stuff.

that's a lot of 0's!

1 trillion = $1,000,000,000,000.

We're constantly bombarded with their ads telling us we *must have* the newest, the latest, the greatest thing.

But guess what? You don't actually need all this new stuff.

Now guess how much money is spent trying to get you to buy something second-hand?

that's NOT a lot of 0's!

$0.

And there's one more very, *very* important reason you should buy stuff that's as good as new:

Buying something second-hand and using it again is

Awesome for the environment.

Less stuff needs to get made. Less pointless packaging. Less stuff thrown out, rotting in a rubbish tip.

Okay, now I'm going to show you how *you* can use the power of **GOOD AS NEW** to make all your Christmases come at once.

How to get what you really want . . . quicker and cheaper

Let's say you put $5 in your **SAVE bucket** every week.

(Remember, every money bucket gets some money every payday.)

Let's look at how many weeks it will take you to save, depending on whether you buy new or second-hand.

	new	GOOD AS NEW
dress	12 weeks ($60)	1 week ($5)
ice-cream machine	26 weeks ($130)	5 weeks ($25)
Treehouse books boxed set	16 weeks ($80)	6 weeks ($30)
bike	60 weeks ($300)	10 weeks ($50)
LEGO Minecraft	25 weeks ($125)	14 weeks ($70)

look how fast you can get stuff!

Here are three things to think about:

First, the only real difference between new and second-hand is the packaging. Think about it —

as soon as you buy something it's *already* second-hand!

Second, with your Barefoot Boss business set up, you'll be able to save for stuff much quicker.

Finally, and most importantly . . .

For the cost of buying a new bike, you could have EVERYTHING on this list (good as new) and still have $80 left over!

SHOW AND TELL

It can be a bit overwhelming to decide what you really want (which is why Santa is such an amazing dude!). On the following pages, you'll meet some kids who share how they used their SAVE buckets to get what they really wanted.

When my friends buy one thing ... I buy ten!

by Mia

AGE: **11**

WHERE: **Queensland**

I love buying stuff I want second-hand because my money goes so much further. You can pick up bargains on places like Facebook Marketplace, and they're honestly as good as new!

With the money I save, I can put more in my GIVE jar. We support Foodbank where they help to feed people in our community. Just $1 makes two meals so a little bit goes a long way.

	new	GOOD AS NEW
rollerskates	$70	$40
ice skates	$100	$40
blow-up kayak	$160	$30
inflatable stand-up paddleboard	$200	$170
LEGO Friends sets (9)	$960	$300
two big bags of second-hand clothes	$300	$30
TOTAL	$1790	$610

That's a BIG difference

I saved $1180!

We scored a great second-hand Switch

by Lachlan

AGE: **10**

WHERE: **New South Wales**

My brother and I wanted a Nintendo Switch more than anything in the world. But the money we were being paid for doing our jobs at home wasn't adding up fast enough, so we started a business cleaning bins.

We made posters and gave them to our neighbours and pretty soon we had clients. We'd grab our walkie-talkies and clean the bins in our street then run home and count our savings. We were making about $20 each most weeks.

We were constantly searching the internet for cheap Nintendo Switches that were either on sale or second-hand. It took us about three months to save enough money, and then one day our hard work and research paid off. We saw a Switch advertised at a second-hand shop. We raced down to the shop and talked them into throwing in a bunch of extra stuff — a case, a game and a memory card — for nothing. It works exactly the same as our friends' Switches, but we saved $220!

$620

I saved $220!

$400

New

Good As New

124

I wanted to make it easier for people to pay

by Oscar

AGE: **10**

WHERE: **Victoria**

I have a muffin stand located in the front yard of our house. We had a lot of tourists in town over the Christmas holidays, and I noticed that most people didn't have cash handy. So with some of my profits I bought a Square reader for $59, which meant I could take card payments. Even though there's a cost to using Square, this investment in my business has paid off! During the next holidays at the local folk festival, in two days I sold over 90 muffins at $3 each! Not many people have cash, so a card reader is a good investment! I've made around $1000 from selling muffins.

> **You've got to spend money to make money!**

Cheap, cheap!
by Allen

AGE: **10**

WHERE: **New South Wales**

I do jam jars at home, and I was saving up for a budgie. But when I went to my local pet store they were charging $210 just for a new cage, *plus* $100 for the budgies! I was really disappointed. It would have taken me way too long to save up just doing chores. So I got on Gumtree and looked, and looked, and looked for over a year! I ended up finding a cage and budgies for $80 total. I saved $230! I named my budgies Ducky and Bluey. Sadly, Bluey flew away, but I still have Ducky!

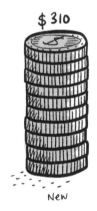

$310

New

I saved $230!

$80

Good As New

Our second-hand best friend!
by Ryder and Alexis

AGE: 9

WHERE: Queensland

We all fell in love with a puppy we found on Facebook Marketplace. The seller had bought it without understanding just how much energy and time it would take up, so he was looking to find it a good home. The puppy was technically second-hand but it was still a lot of money: $2500. Us four kids had to convince our parents that we could look after a puppy – it took a few months. In the end, Mum and Dad said they'd pay half and contributed savings from our bottle collection business (see page 74). Our family grew by one in January 2021, and we all still agree: Nala is the best investment ever!

**" Our dog, Nala,
is our best investment ever! "**

DOGS ARE NOT ONLY YOUR BEST FRIEND, THEY'RE ALSO THE BEST INVESTMENT. WOOF!

127

The chicken, the egg . . . and the hot tub
by Ted and George

AGE: **9 and 7**

WHERE: **South Australia**

We're proud Indigenous kids. We have our own business selling eggs from our six chooks. It's called 'Ted and George's Famous Egg Stall'. When we're saving for something, we put up a picture of our goal in our bedroom and combine our money and work for it together. We try to buy stuff using lay-by, which keeps us motivated. Lay-by is when a shop allows you to make smaller payments, and when it's all paid you can take it home. We've used lay-by to get a new tent, sleeping bags, a cricket bowling machine and an Xbox, and now we're saving up for an $8000 hot tub!

"We love the challenge of saving for our goals!"

128

I bought my very own dream house!
by Emilia

AGE: **6**

WHERE: **Queensland**

I saw a Barbie Dreamhouse in a shop and I really, really wanted one. It had different floors with lights and even an elevator that you can pull up and down with string! But the price was $279, and that was way more than I had in my SAVE jar. So for the rest of the school year I saved hard. I even did extra jobs.

Then one day I looked on Gumtree and saw someone was selling one for $50. We contacted the seller and told them I wanted it, and that I was spending my own money. The lady spoke with her daughter, who was selling the house, and the little girl decided to drop the price to $40 and throw in some extra Barbie clothes because they were both so impressed that a six-year-old had saved that much money. What a bargain!

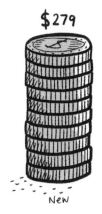

$279

New

I saved $239!

$40

Good As New

129

I'm a rock'n'roll gamer!
by Jarvis

AGE: **14**

WHERE: **Western Australia**

My business is building computers and selling them online – I got the idea when I wanted to buy one and discovered they were really expensive. So I did some research and convinced my parents that I could make a go of building a computer myself. I even sat them down with a PowerPoint presentation with everything I'd found out. They were impressed, and lent me enough money to buy the parts for four computers that I have now built and sold! I have not only managed to pay back my parents, but I bought a second-hand electric guitar for $250 that's worth $1000 new!

$1000

I saved $750!

New

$250

Good As New

Saving is fashionable!
by Ella

AGE: **14**

WHERE: **Victoria**

I'm a natural saver, but it's hard when kids at school always have fashionable and expensive clothes and I don't. I have a business called The SupaSlime Company and I make special recipe slimes so I have my own money but I don't want to spend it all on the latest fashion. So I started searching around in op-shops and vintage clothes shops to find things I like, but for a fraction of the brand-new price. Recycling is good for the environment, and it removes the stress of trying to keep up with my friends. They spend $60 on clothes, I spend $5!

$65

I saved $60!

$5

New

Good As New

I am a dinosaur hunter!
by Archie

AGE: **11**

WHERE: **Victoria**

I've always loved dinosaurs, which is how I got interested in collecting fossils. Did you know that the mosasaurus was the largest dinosaur to have ever lived? It's even bigger than a T-rex! Mosasaurus teeth are pretty rare, so I spent a long time searching on Google and looking at TikTok. I saved up for an entire year, because I knew that when one finally showed up I had to be ready to buy it as it would go very quickly. And it did, because I bought it! It cost me $450, and it's my pride and joy.

❛ Fossils are the ultimate second-hand purchase! ❜

I bought my own boat!
by Maxy

AGE: **15**

WHERE: **Tasmania**

I'd been saving hard and watching Gumtree like a wedge-tailed eagle. Finally, after lots of searching, I got a really cool boat. I named it *Pork Chop*! It's so much fun. My family uses it on the weekend and we even have sleepovers on it . . . and it's so big that the four of us can stay overnight, plus our two dogs! I think real estate is too expensive, so my plan is to live on a houseboat.

$ 25,000

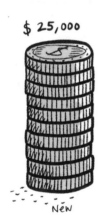

New

I saved $23,000!

$ 2000

Good As New

We saved up and bought a caravan...

by Cody, Annie-Maree and Ashton

AGE: **15, 13 and 9**

WHERE: **New South Wales**

The biggest thing we've bought is a caravan. And it wasn't even for us, it was for our chickens! You may be wondering why chickens need a caravan. It's not for going on holidays, it's for making sure they have somewhere safe and warm to nest and lay their eggs. We pooled our money and it still took us four very long years of saving. We bought it second-hand on Gumtree for $9000 and spent another $2000 renovating it. It's already paid off. Not only have we saved at least $20,000, it's worth more than we paid for it because we gave it a bit of tender loving care and some elbow grease!

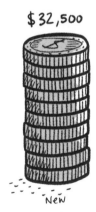

$32,500

New

We saved $21,320!

$11,180

Good As New

Includes $2180 for renovation

134

I paid for an epic family trip!
by Tate

AGE: **9**

WHERE: **Western Australia**

When I was six, I really wanted to go on an adventure. So I saved up for five months and paid for my family to take a day trip to the Pinnacles, which is a desert. It feels like you're on the moon because there are all these epic sandstone pinnacles that have been around for 30,000 years! I paid for entry to the park, and I also bought me and my brother a souvenir from the gift shop. My family said it was the best trip they'd ever been on. And I was super proud to have paid for it myself as a six-year-old!

❝ Think about what you want to spend your savings on. ❞

THE PINNACLES

I have always wanted to go there

Let's find that ONE THING you really want

Okay, you've seen how all these kids decided on their goals, worked and saved hard and made great purchases, with a lot of them buying **good as new**.

Now it's your turn.

write some of your ideas in

PUPPY

fart cushion

DOLL'S HOUSE

COMPUTER

BOAT

WHAT DO REALLY

ROLLERSKATES

CRICKET BAT

TENT

GUITAR

SLEEPING BAG

PASTA MAKER

There are lots of ideas below to get you started. Grab a pencil and add some ideas of your own.

Now I want you to circle **one thing** you would *really* like (and that your parents approve of).

Then I'll show you how to get it quicker than you ever thought possible!

SKATEBOARD

XBOX

SEWING MACHINE

YOU
WANT?

FARTORAMA 2000

COOL CLOTHES

PONY

PHONE

AIR FRYER

BIKE

HOLIDAY

NINTENDO SWITCH

TOP 5 TIPS

Be an online shopping superstar

1 **Get your parents' help**
You'll probably need to use your parents' account to search for stuff and make offers. You'll also need their card to pay for whatever you buy (but you'll pay them back!).

2 **Do your research**
Read online reviews. Often you can find last year's model, good as new, which is sometimes *better* than the new one! Then check out Facebook Marketplace, Gumtree, eBay and Google to find the lowest price.

3 **Always offer a lower price**
On second-hand websites, people **ALWAYS** ask for a cheaper price. A good starting point is to offer 25% less than the price they listed. Then say politely: 'I'm ____ years old and I've saved up for this from my own business. Would you take ____ ?' You can always go higher if they don't accept your offer.

4 **If you have to, buy it new**
If you really can't find it second-hand, you can still save money. Just google the product name and search for the lowest prices, but make sure you compare prices that *include* delivery. Watch out for '$1 teddy bear for sale, $100 postage!'.

5 **Search for the code**
When you're at the checkout page, you may see a box called 'discount code'. Always search for the discount code or coupon (e.g. 'LEGO Discount Code'). There are heaps of websites that track these codes, and they can save you lots of money.

IT'S TIME TO TURBO CHARGE THINGS!

We've been talking about buying things cheaply.

Now we are going to talk about selling things to get some

QUICK CASH!

Let's say you've decided your savings goal is to buy a bike.

A new bike costs $300, and it could take you well over a year to save up for it.

Here's what you do. Start searching online and find the same bike **as good as new** for $50, listed on an online marketplace. You might find one at a garage sale or an op-shop.

$50 . . . this means you'll be able to buy the bike in the next few months – not next year!

Awesome, right?

Sure, but I want you to buy it *even faster.*

 I want you to have a good look at all the stuff in the room you're in.

Go on.

The average family has $5400 worth of stuff just lying around their house, stuff they no longer use (according to figures from Gumtree).

And in the next five minutes you're going to turn some of that stuff into treasure by selling it. Then you'll use the money you get to buy <u>what you *really* want</u>.

This is seriously easy to do (as long as you get permission from your parents to sell stuff). In fact, this is exactly how Liam (see page 82) made **$3500** from stuff in his bedroom!

Ready?

This is the ultimate treasure hunt!

I don't want this to be a drag. It can't be boring. It needs to be done quickly. So, first, set an alarm for five minutes.

With the clock ticking, I want you to go on a treasure hunt around your house. You're searching for two or three things you no longer use.

Keep an eye out for:

★ good-as-new clothes you've grown out of

★ electronics that are packed away in a cupboard

★ toys and musical instruments that no-one uses anymore.

Ready, set,
GO FIND SOME TREASURE!

Did you find something to sell?

Place whatever unused treasure you've found on the kitchen table.

Then ask your parents for permission to sell this stuff. They are in control, so what they say goes (and if you haven't found anything, you could ask for their suggestions).

Next, **it's time to do some research.** Grab an iPad or your parent's phone.

You're looking for two prices:

First, how much the item you're selling costs brand new.
Type it into Google and hit the **shopping** icon.

Second, how much the item is selling for second-hand on Gumtree.

Example:

Guitar (new): $300 ⟶ **Gumtree:** $100
Saving: $200

WARNING: You'll be shocked at how much the price drops.

Yet that's a good thing! Because you're going to be both selling *and* buying stuff.

Once you see for yourself how much the price drops straight after you buy it, you will never again be sucked into advertising that tries to make you spend all your hard-earned cash on new stuff.

And even better: you've done something awesome for the environment . . . **twice!**

Bottom line: nearly everything you want is right now sitting in someone else's house gathering dust.

Now, let me show you how to sell it online like a pro . . .

TOP 5 TIPS

Be an online super-seller

1 **Get your parents' permission**
You'll need them to register for a selling account, and possibly to talk to potential buyers.

2 **Always take too many photos**
Buyers appreciate being able to look at lots of photos (especially any scratches, marks or dents).

3 **Be honest and up-front**
If there's anything wrong with what you're selling, mention it in your description and show it in your photos. Not only is it the right thing to do, it makes people trust you more!

4 **Set your price high**
Always do your research to see what similar items are going for. Buyers will ALWAYS ask for a discount, so make sure you list a price that's higher than you want to get.

5 **Sell on different sites**
The more places you list your item, the more buyers you'll attract. Most sites are free, so list your item on Gumtree, Facebook Marketplace and eBay. You could also consider holding a garage sale or a suitcase rummage (see Hannah's story on page 100).

You're probably thinking . . .

Where do you buy good-as-new stuff?

Talk to your parents to see if they'll let you check out Facebook Marketplace, Gumtree or eBay (in most cases you'll need them to register for an account).

Otherwise, going to an op-shop or a local garage sale is a great way to go on a mystery shopping tour where you'll find hidden gems at very, very low prices.

I can't find what I really want second-hand.

That's okay!

You don't need to buy everything good as new, and sometimes finding exactly what you want can be hard. So, when that happens, google to find the cheapest price you can. Don't forget to add in the cost of shipping (which can add to the cost of buying stuff online).

It says I have to be 18 to register for eBay and Gumtree. Plus I don't have a Facebook account!

That's why you should use your parents' account, or have them register for one. It's also why you need to have your parents on board with this, because they'll probably need to help you interact with the buyers. Remember, you can also hold a garage sale or do a suitcase rummage.

I can't find anything to sell.

Did you know that the average 10-year-old kid has 238 toys . . .
but only plays with 12? (That's what a survey of British kids found,
but I think it's pretty accurate for Australia as well.)

My advice?

Stop thinking about what you're giving up (the stuff in your cupboard
gathering dust!) and start thinking about the things you really want.

What about buying stuff online like Roblox, PokéCoins or V-Bucks?

Those smaller things come out of your SPLURGE bucket.

What I want costs too much.

You're wanting to buy the world's most advanced fart machine,
aren't you?

Look, the Fartorama 2000 is a very expensive machine, and that's
why I suggest you talk to your parents about what you want,
and make sure they approve.

If it's really expensive they might suggest you make it a joint savings
goal with your brother or sister. Or your parents might chip in some
money if you save up a certain amount (although, let's face it,
it's unlikely they'll agree to funding the Fartorama 2000).

You've been working very hard.

Your buckets are filling up nicely.

You have plans and goals for your **SAVE** bucket.

You've turbocharged your savings by selling stuff you no longer use: that's a **BIG WIN.**

And in no time, you'll have what you want.

"We think our chicken caravan is really cool and, even better, it helps us to make more money!!"

Cody, Annie-Maree and Ashton

YOU ROCK!

Santa must be sweating right now (and not just because he's carrying a few kilos).

You're one of the very few kids who's worked out how to get what you want!

Go to the back of the book and get this sticker:

Stick it on the chart on page 23. Well done!

You don't have to wait around all year to find out what Santa left you . . . you now know how to get any present you can think of, and you can make it happen.

No chimneys or reindeers required!

(Okay, of course you're still going to be super interested in what Santa brings!)

However, you're one smart cookie: businesses can spend mountains of money trying to convince you to spend your hard-earned money on new stuff, but you've worked out how to buy 'better than new'.

Plus, you've done something awesome for the environment . . . **twice!**

Next up, I'm going to show you the superpower of the **GIVE** bucket.

This is the step that will change the way people look at you . . . and how you look at yourself.

STEP 5

MAKE
SOMEONE
SMILE

Most kids would have totally given up by now . . .

But Not You.

And that's why I know you're ready for this step.

I'm going to show you how to make people smile, by spreading kindness.

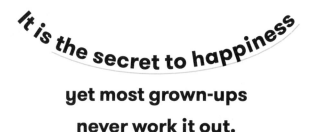

It is the secret to happiness

yet most grown-ups

never work it out.

I'm going to:

★ show you how to be a superhero to your family and friends

★ introduce you to a boy who adopted a koala

★ show you how you can feed a family in need

★ reveal the **BEST PRESENT** you'll ever get.

(Oh, and you're also going to have a fist fight . . . with yourself.)

Right now, let's meet a girl who . . . built a school!

The eight-year-old who helped build a school

Amalia lives in Adelaide with her mum and brothers and sisters. Her favourite thing to do is to ride horses, which she does each week.

She also loves fashion and has designed 12 dresses, which she sells at local markets and online.

Yet there's something amazing about what Amalia has done with the money she puts in her **GIVE bucket:**

She built a school.

SERIOUSLY.

Amalia (with her mum, Susan) was given a piece of her grandmother's land and built a three-storey school. It has three classrooms on each level and a big dance hall at the bottom.

It took a long time to build, but it's now home to 120 primary school students.

But there's something **even more amazing** about the school Amalia helped to build . . .

ADELAiDE
(AUSTRALiA)

It's in Kenya, Africa, in a place called Korogocho. Korogocho is a Swahili word that means 'shoulder to shoulder' . . . and that's how people live in Korogocho.

Amalia told me about going over to meet her relatives who live in Korogocho. She hung out with her cousins at her auntie's house.

'Their house is made of tin, kind of like a small garden shed, with dirt floors. It's just one little room that is smaller than our bathroom. There is no kitchen. No lounge room. And **there's only one bed . . . FOR SIX PEOPLE!'**

Oh, and there's **NO TOILET.**

'The toilet is down the road, and it's just a hole in the ground, and it stinks. And the poo and wee is *everywhere*. People walk through it. It's disgusting!'

In Korogocho there isn't much electricity, so it gets really dark inside. There are no air conditioners. Lots of strangers have to share one tap for water.

Many kids there can't afford to go to school, and those who do are stuck in a classroom that can have as many as 150 kids!

Yes, life in Korogocho is tough.

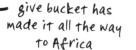
money from Amalia's give bucket has made it all the way to Africa

KOROGOCHO
(KENYA)

The kids who are Amalia's age play in a creek that is polluted with rubbish and sewage.

'For fun they find old bike tyres and use them as hula hoops,' says Amalia.

Amalia and her mum set out to do something for the kids of Korogocho.

They are not rich, but they paid for the school themselves from their GIVE buckets.

Now the school is up and running, they are paying the wages of six teachers and three helpers. The kids get cooked lunches and the chance to learn dancing and all the important stuff that kids need to learn.

'I'm proud of our school. If we hadn't built it, none of those kids would have gone to school,' Amalia says. 'The reason my **GIVE bucket** is so important to me is that my goal in life is to **make the world kinder**.'

MAKE THE WORLD A KINDER PLACE

Let me tell you my own story

I used to get really down . . . mostly because I compared myself to other kids and I felt like I was a failure . . . and that **everyone else was better than me**. Faster than me. **More popular than me**. Smarter than me.

So I tried to make myself feel better by having the latest stuff. And it worked for a little while. I'd get super-excited about the brand new thing I'd bought. Even better, other kids would see this cool thing and want to play with me.

But that feeling always wore off pretty quickly, and then I'd be back to feeling frustrated and unpopular. And then something happened at school that changed everything.

'Your assignment is to write someone's life story,' said my teacher.

Most kids just interviewed their parents, but I decided to find someone even older than them. I stopped by the local old people's home and asked the nurse at the front desk if she could help me. 'I have just the person, come with me,' she said.

She introduced me to Jack, who looked like he was 100 years old. It was kind of awkward, because he was stooped over and he mumbled so it was hard to make out what he was saying.

Yet when I started to listen to Jack, I realised he was actually pretty interesting. Over the next few weeks I worked really hard and wrote his life story.

And guess what?

The teacher gave me an

I was pretty happy with that

But you know what the best part was?

When I read Jack his story, he had tears in his eyes.

'You've made a lonely old man very happy,' he said.

That was when it hit me:

THE FASTEST WAY TO FEEL GOOD IS TO **HELP OTHER PEOPLE**

I realised that if I stopped feeling sorry for myself and started focusing on making other people feel good . . . pretty soon I felt good too.

And that's what this step is all about.

You don't need to do something as epic as building a school to **MAKE A DIFFERENCE** to someone else's life.

Superheroes don't use their fists

Some people want to hold on to all their money. They don't want to share it with anyone.

I get it: you've **worked hard** so you think you should be able to keep it all for yourself.

I want you to do me a favour and clench your fist.

Go on, do it. Clench your fist as tight as you can. Please keep reading, and hold your fist tight until I tell you to stop.

Okay, so have a look at your hand. It's starting to feel uncomfortable and you're stressed, right?

(Keep holding your fist tight!)

A clenched fist sends the signal to your body and your brain that you're **not happy**. That you might be a bit *angry*.

Is your hand starting to hurt now?

A lot of people have a clenched fist when it comes to spending their money . . . they don't want to let any of it go, especially to anyone else.

I bet your hand is *really* hurting now.

Okay, so now I want you to *relax* your hand. Open your hand up.

It feels so . . . peaceful, right?

An open hand is the universal signal of kindness. It's welcoming.
It's a high-five. It's a pat on the back. It's shaking hands. It's holding
hands. It's how you make friends.

When you hang on to your money tightly, you're probably only
thinking about yourself and your problems and what you might buy
to make yourself feel better.

But here's the thing:

The stuff you buy
doesn't make you happy.

Helping people makes you happy.

Once you open your hand and start **GIVING**, you'll find it hard to stop!

The best present ever

Let me tell you about the best present I ever received.

My uncle arrived at our farm with a black dog. 'I have no use for this dog on my farm, so I'm going to give her to you,' he said kindly. 'I call her Betty.'

No-one knew exactly how old Betty was because she'd been passed from farmer to farmer for years.

That first night, I put her food in a shiny new doggy bowl. Betty cocked her head and wouldn't eat it. Perhaps she was nervous in a new place, and off her food?

My uncle had another idea. 'Just tip the food on the ground,' he said.

So I did, and she immediately started chowing down.

Betty wasn't used to being treated with kindness.

Yet over the next few months she became a member of our family.

We played with her.
We cuddled her.
We bought her treats.

Well, Betty repaid our kindness by becoming the hardest working sheep dog we'd ever had on our farm. She outworked three dogs!

It's like a ripple of kindness happened:

My uncle did a kind act by giving us Betty . . .

Then we showed Betty love and kindness . . .

And then Betty worked hard because her dream had come true –
she had a home and a family that loved her.

That's how kindness works. You do one small act for someone and then
they do something for another person and **everyone feels good**.

You feel good when you do good things for other people.

Now you're going to use the money in your GIVE bucket to start your
own ripple of kindness.

KINDNESS IS A SUPER POWER

ACTS OF KINDNESS

I want you to think of one person who you could make smile. Who could you do an **Act of Kindness** for?

You could buy your mum some flowers. Or take your dad out for hot chocolate. You could buy a plant for your grandmother (and then you could plant it together). You could give your annoying little sister a treat.

Now, this is important:

It's not about the amount of money you spend . . .
$1 to $5 is more than enough.

The most important thing is

the time and effort you put in.

That's what will make someone smile.

Write down some of your own ideas

Who would I like to be kind to?

It could be someone you know, or a charity . . .

....
....
....
....

What could I do?

It doesn't need to be big – just make someone smile . . .

....
....
....

How much will it cost?

Sometimes, the best ideas are free . . .

....
....
....
....

STOP If you just skimmed over the **Acts of Kindness** on the previous page, I want you to go back and fill in some ideas.

Then I want you to picture the person whose name is at the top of the list.

Close your eyes for a few seconds and imagine the smile on their face when you give them your amazingly thoughtful present and homemade card. Or you do something special for them.

When you give your first gift of kindness, you'll soon find something out for yourself:

It's much more exciting **TO GIVE** than it is to recieve a gift.

Over time, being kind is what makes you popular. It's what people will love about you.

It's time to turbocharge kindness!

Okay, you've done your **Act of Kindness**, and I bet you feel really good.

Now you're ready to take the next step ... where you'll do something amazing (like Amalia, who built a school).

Here's how you're going to do it.

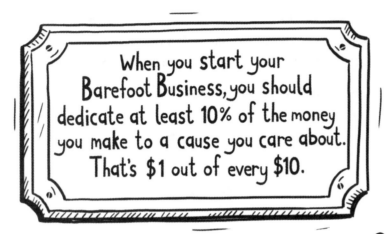

When you start your Barefoot Business, you should dedicate at least 10% of the money you make to a cause you care about. That's $1 out of every $10.

In other words, you are starting a business with a purpose. You're going to make a difference.

Some of the money from your business could:

⭐ feed a hungry family

⭐ pay the vet bill to save a sick dog

⭐ buy the only present a little kid gets on Christmas Day.

Seriously, how cool is that?

Oh, and make sure you tell your customers . . .

Your customers will love it when they hear that you're not just in business for yourself — you're here to change the world.

So you need to let them know.

When you get to the end of the book (page 217) you'll find a Barefoot Kids Certificate to fill in. This will let your customers know all the good things you're supporting through your business.

After a hard day's work, you'll know that:

 You helped your customers.

 You made some money.

 You helped to make a difference!

How good is that?

Alright, so now you're probably thinking:

'How do I decide who to give my money to?'

On the following pages, you'll meet some kids who are using their GIVE buckets to do some seriously epic stuff.

I adopted a koala
by Xavier

AGE: **6**

WHERE: **Queensland**

Photo courtesy of Paradise Country

I remember watching the 2019 Black Summer bushfires on TV and seeing all the injured koalas. It made me so upset that I demanded my parents drive to the fires to help the koalas! With the pocket money I saved, I bought $100 worth of towels and donated them to the Currumbin Wildlife Sanctuary. I have a business making 'spooky boo' jars for Halloween that I sold at a Kids Take Over market. I use my GIVE bucket money to sponsor a koala named Niley through the Australian Koala Foundation. It costs $30 a month. Niley was a joey when I started sponsoring her, and she recently had her own baby called Nellie! She's so cute! I visit Nellie and other koalas like Mirri (in the photo) at Paradise Country on the Gold Coast.

While I'm saving up to go to Jurassic Park in Hawaii, I'm also saving koalas.

I bought socks
for homeless people
by Olivia

AGE: **10**

WHERE: **Tasmania**

I started my own business in December 2021 making face masks, headbands, tote bags and bookmarks. I taught myself to sew with the help of Google and YouTube. I love helping to save the environment with reusable masks, but my most important bucket is the GIVE bucket. I donate a third of the money I make to help people in my community: for every $10 sale I give $3.

I live in Hobart, Tasmania, and it gets really cold. Can you imagine how freezing it would be if you were homeless in winter? So I used the money from my GIVE jar to buy 134 pairs of socks to donate to the Hobart City Mission. They handed them out to homeless people so they could keep their feet warm. I'm a good Barefooter!

"We can all change the world – one step at a time."

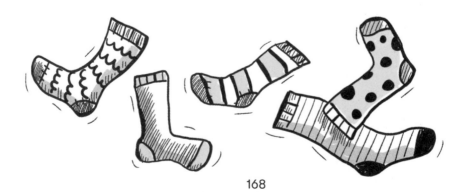

We feed a family in Cambodia
by Indiana and Summer

AGE: **9 and 12**

WHERE: **South Australia**

We have a business with Poppy (our grandpa) that we call 'Garnish'. We sell dehydrated oranges, lemons and limes that people use in their cooking and drinks. We ask family and friends for fruit from their trees or buy it cheap from the local farmers' market. Then Poppy dehydrates it, and we package it to sell at our local market. We love having a business with Poppy because when he drops off the fruit at our house we get to hang out and see him.

We give 10% of the money we make to Transform Cambodia, a charity that our school supports. Our money provides a family in Cambodia with food and education. It's pretty cool we can do that. And Poppy is so proud!

> **Being generous is important – you don't want to be greedy and keep everything for yourself.**

We buy Christmas presents for other kids

by Maisie and Poppy

AGE: **9 and 8**

WHERE: **New South Wales**

We collect recyclable cans and
bottles from neighbours and friends,
then return them and get paid!
We use our SAVE jar for things
like teddies and a doll's pram.
At Christmastime Mum takes us
shopping and we use our GIVE jars
to buy toys for kids whose parents don't have any money. We add our
gifts to the Wishing Tree Appeal in Kmart. It makes us feel really proud
that kids will wake up on Christmas Day and unwrap the presents we
bought them and they'll have big smiles on their faces.

> **Believe in yourself and you will make
> lots of money for all your jars.**

I'm a dog walker with a purpose
by Zoe

AGE: 12

WHERE: New South Wales

I've always wanted a dog, so when I was 10 I decided to start my own dog-walking business so I could hang out with dogs! I've saved up for half of a second-hand bike ($150) and half of an Xbox ($350) as well as clothes and other things. I have donated almost $1000 to Guide Dogs Australia with the money in my GIVE bucket. They have a Puppy Pals program where I get regular updates on how these super-cute puppies are doing. At home it's my job to gather cans and plastic to recycle and we donate the proceeds to WIRES Wildlife Rescue. My dream is to become a guide dog puppy raiser one day!

> **I love seeing how the guide dogs are going, knowing I've made a contribution.**

MY GUIDE DOG BUDDIES HELP A LOT OF PEOPLE.

I give food
by Kami

AGE: **11**

WHERE: **Queensland**

When the floods hit Australia in 2022
I saw how many people had lost their
homes. My music teacher's house got
flooded so she wasn't at school, and
I wondered what I could do to help.
So Mum and I opened up the pantry
and filled a box to the brim and drove
it to a local evacuation centre, which wasn't
far from our house. The people there were really grateful for the food.
We also held a garage sale and donated the money to Foodbank and
OzHarvest. No-one should go hungry.

**❛ Everyone can find some way of
helping other people who are in need. ❜**

I give for my mum's memory
by Ollie

AGE: **12**

WHERE: **Victoria**

I'm a big cricket fan, so I decided to create my own cricket-themed card game, which I call 'First XI Cricket'. The game uses real player test match statistics, which I researched myself. My sisters helped me to trial the game until I got it right.

My game got featured on television and it blew up — we did $30,000 in sales, including to the Australian cricket team! Mum was really sick with cancer for about five years before she died in 2020. I was so pleased to be able to donate 50% of my profits to the Cancer Council.

My sisters and I want to do everything we can to find a cure for cancer – my younger sister ran 10 kilometres on her tenth birthday and raised $10,000. We all cheered her on. I think Mum would be proud of us.

I am really proud of finding a way to make a difference.

I can't think of an Act of Kindness I'd like to do!

Okay, start with your mum. Tell her you'd like to take her out to a cafe for hot chocolate and you're going to pay. Trust me, she'll love it (plus you get hot chocolate).

Know this: you don't have to spend lots of money on a present. You could make something. Or you could go to an op-shop and buy something and wrap it. What makes a present special is the thought you put into it: that's what the person remembers.

WARNING: Being kind is addictive. It'll make you feel great and you'll want to keep doing it.

How do I choose between doing an Act of Kindness and supporting a cause?

Easy. Think of it like this.

The money you get from Payday Jobs is split into your three buckets. (Remember the rule: each money bucket gets at least some money every payday.) You can use the money you put into your GIVE bucket to do the Acts of Kindness that you put on your list on page 163.

When it comes to supporting a cause, that money will come from your Barefoot Boss business. You can donate 10% of the money you make to the charity you choose. That's $1 out of every $10 you make.

Can you help me think of a cause?

Here are three ideas:

First, you could choose a charity that's related to your business. Like Zoe does – she's a dog walker and gives money to Guide Dogs Australia. Or, if you have a food stall, you could choose to give some money to Foodbank, which provides food for hungry families.

Second, you could raise some money for your school. Bonus: it'll make your principal and teachers very happy!

Third, you could take part in a Christmas appeal and buy presents for kids in need (like Maisie and Poppy who take part in Kmart's Wishing Tree Appeal). Not only is it lots of fun to go shopping, you might be providing the only present a little kid gets on Christmas Day. How good would that feel?

Can I donate my time instead?

Absolutely! Perhaps you could volunteer to stack some boxes at Foodbank (do this with your parents). Or maybe you could take out the bins for an older person who lives in your street. Remember, it's not the amount of money you spend, but the time and effort you put in.

But I don't want to share my money!

Well, I can't make you do it.

However, what I can tell you is that you're really going to be missing out.

After all, giving is the fastest way to make yourself happier.

Besides, why would you want to walk around with a clenched fist all the time?

Are you smarter than a 38-year-old?

The answer is probably **YES!**

You understand how to set up and use your money buckets, which means you're going to be a way better money manager than most adults (remember, they're walking around with leaky buckets).

You are using your **SPLURGE** bucket for little things you want.

You are stashing money in your **SAVE** bucket for your big goals.

And now you know that your **GIVE** bucket is for making people smile . . .

And you've unlocked a very big secret:

kindness is your superpower!

'Don't let your parents tell you they are too busy to support you changing the world. They need to make time! '

Amalia

CONGRATULATIONS!

You have worked out how to make people smile, and now your family and friends will look at you differently.

Even more importantly, you will look at *yourself* differently.

You've written down some Acts of Kindness that you can do.

And you've chosen a cause you believe in, and now you're going to roll up your sleeves and make a difference.

Most adults never get around to doing stuff like this.

Go to the back of the book and get this sticker:

Stick it on the chart on page 23.

You should feel proud of yourself.

Next up, I'm going to show you something that most grown-ups think of as 'magic'.

Soon you'll be able to walk into a supermarket and say to the cashier:

'Did you know I own this business?'

STEP 6

GROW YOUR MONEY

You've made it all the way to the back of this book . . .

to our final step!

You are ready.

See, our final step is a very special one: I'm going to show you how to *grow* your money.

Some adults think this step is about 'magic' . . .
but it's really just about being smart with your money.

I'll let you into a secret:

Growing your money is like any other skill you can learn.

And that's why **every grown-up wishes they could be you right now**, sitting down with me, about to learn one of the most magical skills in life . . . while you're still a kid.

In the next few pages you're going to:

★ meet a nine-year-old who owns part of a Bunnings store

★ discover how you can own part of McDonald's, Nintendo and Minecraft for as little as $5

★ meet a 13-year-old who learnt the magical steps to growing her money in the time it takes to make a cheese toastie!

Plus, we'll plant a few . . . **apple trees!**

LET'S GROW...

You're just a kid . . . how do you own <u>THAT?</u>

One day at our local Coles, I proudly told the lady at the checkout:

'You know, I actually own part of this store.'

She stopped scanning and stared at me like I was a wonky wheel on a shopping trolley.

'WHAT? But you're just a *kid*! How can you own part of this supermarket?'

She didn't believe me.

Yet I was telling the truth.

And it'll soon be true for you too . . .

Throughout the following pages, you'll meet some kids who are growing their money.

Introducing . . .

a brand new money bucket!

So you've been working your way through the steps . . .

You've been doing your jobs around the house . . . putting some money every week into your three money buckets: **SPLURGE, SAVE** and **GIVE**.

✓ You've become a Barefoot Boss . . .
and you've turbocharged your savings.

✓ You've made a difference
by doing Acts of Kindness!

Now it's time to learn how to be really smart with your money. And you're going to do something really cool!

You're ready to set up an extra bucket that you need to put some money into each payday.

But here's the difference. Every dollar that you decide to put into your **GROW** bucket . . . umm, grows.

Think of your GROW bucket like a popcorn machine that pops out brand new $1 coins.

183

How the GROW bucket works

When you wanted to earn *more* money than your pocket money jobs, what did you do?

You became a **Barefoot Boss** and started your own little business!

That's because having your own business gives you the opportunity to make a *lot* more money.

Well, did you know that you can buy a tiny part of huge businesses?

Like, say, McDonald's, Coles, Nintendo and Minecraft.

It's called 'investing', and it basically means you can buy a tiny **share** of these big businesses in your **GROW** bucket . . . and you can get started with as little as $5! (And then you add more money as you get the hang of it.)

GROW bucket = investing apps

Here's you: 'So how do I choose which companies to invest in?'

Here's me: 'You don't. Instead, you get experts to do the choosing for you.'

Here's you: 'Phew! So how do I find these experts?'

Here's me: 'Easy. They all have apps that you can download.'

There are lots of **investing apps** that hold *shares* in the biggest companies in Australia and the world.

So, all *you* need to do is sign up to one of these investing apps, and they'll do the investing for you.

Even better, there are some investing apps that are especially designed for kids. This means you can start to grow your money with just $5! (Different apps require different start-off amounts, but most are under $50.)

I'll show you how to set up your GROW bucket in 15 minutes on page 202.

How do you make money out of shares?

Well, when the big businesses you own a tiny share of do well, they share some of the money they make with you.

In fact, have a look at the chart below.

It shows that, over a very long time (120 years!),

$1 invested in shares

has grown to

$788,013!

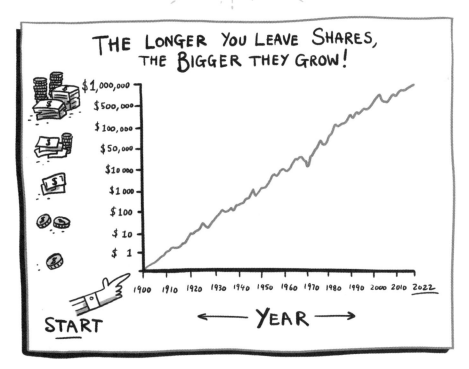

Source: Bloomberg, ASX, RBA, AMP (Data shown is for Australian shares prior to any fees and taxes)

Remember this . . .

Here are the main take-outs about growing your money:

1 Your GROW bucket is for
growing your money!

2 You grow your money by setting up
an investing app on your parents' phone.

3 The investing app invests in shares of huge businesses,
and they pay you money when they make money.

Your money actually works for you while you're sleeping!

This is how your money grows over the years.

And that's how you get what you want!

The super-duper brag

In a moment I'll show you how to set up your investing app, and then how to buy shares. But first, here's a small taste of the kinds of businesses you'll be able to brag to your family and friends that you own.

In fact, let's look at a typical day and see how many times you could say: 'I own part of that.

You wake up and have cereal that was bought from either **Coles** or **Woolies.** You own shares in both.

Then you get dressed and pull on your shoes. You own **Nike** shares.

You have a bit of time before school so you decide to annoy your sister by firing your Nerf gun at her Barbie dolls. You own shares in the companies that make **Nerf guns** *and* **Barbies.**

Your mum drives you to school in her Toyota. You own **Toyota** shares. She taps your lunch order on her iPhone. You own **Apple** shares (and you also own shares in **Telstra,** which provides the internet service). When you get to school you do a research assignment and look things up on Google. You own shares in **Google** . . . and **YouTube**!

Dad picks you up from school in his Ford. You own shares in **Ford**.
For a treat he takes you through the Macca's drive-through. You own
shares in **McDonald's**. You get a Happy Meal that comes with a Coke.
You own shares in **Coca-Cola**.

When you get home, you flick on your Kogan television. You own
Kogan shares. You jump on Netflix. You own shares in **Netflix** . . .
but then you switch over to Disney+. You own shares in **Disney**.
Finally, you decide to play on your Xbox. You own shares in **Microsoft**,
which owns Xbox (and **Minecraft!**).

When you put $5 in your GROW bucket, you can own a small share
of these huge businesses. (I'll explain *how* you can own all these
companies in a moment. Hint: all you'll need is $5 . . . and your parents'
phone.)

These big businesses *pay you* money when they make money.
Without you having to do *any work*.

How brag-worthy is that?

I own part of that

I own part of that

I own part of that

and part of these

189

I own Bunnings!
by Toby

AGE: **9**

WHERE: **Queensland**

I love going to Bunnings on the weekend with Mum and Dad. So I did some research and found out that Bunnings is owned by a company called Wesfarmers, and that I could buy their shares. So I saved up money from doing chores, and with some help from Mum and Dad I bought $500 worth of their shares. I feel really proud because most kids don't own shares. And it's a great business — everyone goes to Bunnings on the weekend, even if it's just for the sausages. Now I own part of Bunnings, so I get paid when they make money. And they make a lot of it!

Keep doing your jobs and save as much as you can. And spend your money on things you really want.

What's the big deal about growing your money?

You may be wondering why you'd put off spending money now, to have more later.

So let me count the ways:

1 because when you put money into your **GROW** bucket it works for you.

2 because it's just heaps of fun, *and* your friends will think you're a money genius.

3 because it gives you a massive head start on saving up for really big things.

Like what?

Like eventually buying a house, or a car, or even a fancy island.

Who knows?

Start putting money into your GROW bucket NOW!

Here's a story that explains how you can get a head start that most grown-ups would envy.

Meet Michelle and Daniel, two pimply 15-year-olds.

Michelle starts putting $100 into her GROW bucket every month for 10 years. After 10 years, she stops, and lets her GROW bucket do the work.

At the same time Michelle stops, Daniel starts. He's 25 years old.

Just like Michelle, Daniel invests $100 a month. Yet unlike Michelle, he doesn't stop — he keeps going for another 35 years.

In total, Michelle puts $12,000 into her GROW bucket, while Daniel puts in $42,000.

Now I have a question for you:

Who will have more money when they're old and grey (aged 60)?

Daniel right? After all, he's put in four times as much money.

Actually, no.

Daniel will have . . . **$379,664.**

Michelle will have . . . **$668,570!**

Whaaat??? How is this possible?

Well, it's called 'compound interest'.

← *You don't need to know the maths – just that it works*

The point is,

the longer you leave your money in your GROW bucket, the more it grows!

that is why it is called a GROW bucket!

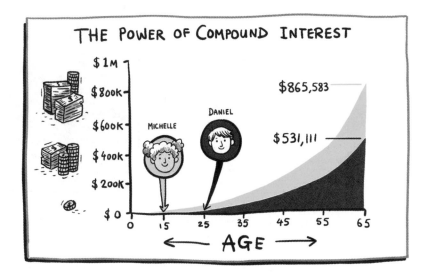

This is why you need to start NOW.

Yet I saved the best for last:

You're probably younger than 15 right now.

Imagine how far ahead in the race you'll be if you start right NOW!

When you learn **how to grow your money** you'll *never* be broke. And you'll always be able to help out your family and friends if they hit hard times.

You will be the superhero, because you have

super investing powers!

My goal is to take care of my family!

by Finnion

AGE: **12**

WHERE: **Queensland**

My parents are big Barefoot fans and they shared the adult Barefoot Investor book with me. Even though I was still a little kid at the time, one thing I loved was the idea of growing my money by investing in shares. As soon as I read about it, I was determined to buy shares of my own

But I was only getting paid $9 a week from my jobs. So I'd also do stuff for friends and family to earn extra money. And I'd ask that all birthday and Christmas presents were put towards me buying shares. Shares are the best present, because they pay me money every year!

And I get really excited every time a company pays me money, because I use the money to buy more shares. So my money grows. I like feeling financially safe and in control. My goal is to one day be rich enough to take care of my family and others.

> **I now ask for money for shares for Christmas and birthdays. I save up for things like LEGO Minecraft and buy it second-hand.**

Let me tell you a secret . . .

Some people might tell you that investing is risky, and that they're too scared to invest.

Why?

Because the price of shares can go up and down (kind of like food prices at the supermarket).

Yet here's the secret: the reason they're scared is that, unlike you, no-one has ever sat down and shown them how shares really work.

Whenever I get upset or scared about something, my dad always says to me:

'Don't worry. **She'll be apples, mate!**'

At first I had no idea what he was talking about . . . why would everything be apples?

It was only later that I found out that 'she'll be apples, mate' is an old Aussie saying that means:

Everything is going to be alright.

Yet what I didn't know is that Dad was teaching me a huge lesson in how to invest my money . . . and make sure everything in my life was going to be alright.

So now I'm going to show you how shares work (with a little help from Dad).

The apple tree story

Growing apples is a super-easy way to learn how to grow your money.

First, I want you to understand that your **GROW** bucket works the same way that an apple tree does: you put in a little bit of money now, and your money will grow just like apples do on an apple tree . . .

Let's say your mum takes you down to Bunnings and buys you an apple tree. It's tiny! (About the size of a dunny brush.) You head home, go out to the backyard, and find a nice sunny spot. You dig a hole and plant the tiny tree in the ground. And sprinkle a bit of worm juice and chook poop on the soil.
And then you basically forget about it . . .
while the apple tree starts growing.

A few years goes by and you notice that your little apple tree has grown – it's now as tall as you. And it's produced a couple of hard little sour apples.

A few more years go by. You walk past the apple tree and you notice it's really shot up: it's now taller than your dad! Even better, it's got heaps of bright, red, juicy apples. You pick one. Crunch! It's delicious!

Then, when you're all grown-up, you walk out to your backyard and see that your apple

tree is now humongous! You stretch your neck up, up, up, and look to the top of the tree. It's taller than your house! And across its huge thick branches there are hundreds and hundreds of juicy apples. You start picking the apples and putting them into a basket: there are way too many for you to eat, so you can share them with your family and friends.

The moral of the story is . . .

from little things, BIG THINGS GROW!

When you planted the apple tree in your backyard it was tiny – the size of a dunny brush – with no apples.

Yet the longer you left the apple tree to grow . . . the more apples you got each year! Remember, it only took a few minutes to plant the tree when you were a little kid . . . and then it kept growing and growing and growing.

In other words:

the longer you leave the money in your GROW bucket, the more it grows.

Why every grown-up wants to be **YOU** right now

Most grown-ups didn't learn how to grow their money until they were much, much older.

Think about someone your parents' age planting a little apple tree. They don't have as much time as you do, so they get a bit frustrated.

They plant it, and then stand back with their hands on their hips and yell at the tree:

'Where are my flipping apples? Come on! I'm hungry now! Grow!'

Each day they walk out to the backyard and stare at the tree, checking to see if there are any apples.

(There aren't any.)

They worry that it's not growing any apples because the dog is lifting its leg and peeing on the trunk. Or maybe the tree's in the wrong spot? So they pull it up and plant it over the other side of the yard where it's (maybe) sunnier. Finally, after a few months with no apples, they yank the tree out and plant another one . . . and start all over again.

That will never happen to you . . .

THE BEST TIME TO PLANT YOUR APPLE TREE IS

NOW!

Get a head start on everyone else.

By the time you get to your parents' age your apple tree will be HUGE. You could attach a swing seat in the branches and have tons of apples to eat, bake into pies, and share with your family and friends! And you get more and more each year.

Shares grow like apple trees

Growing your money is like growing an apple tree:
the main ingredient is time, and you've got lots of it.

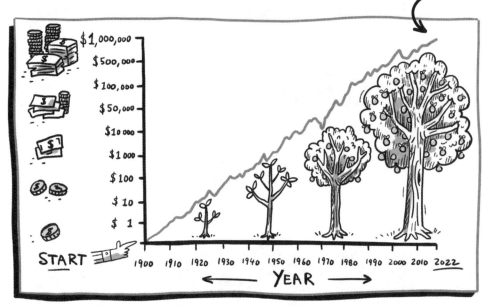

$788,013 (11.8%.pa)
value of $1 invested
in Jan 1900

Source: Bloomberg, ASX, RBA, AMP (Data shown is for Australian shares prior to any fees and taxes)

The three lessons the apple tree can teach you about investing:

1 If you set up your GROW bucket,
your money will grow like magic!

2 The earlier you start, the more money
you'll have later on.

3 If you pull the money out of your
GROW bucket you'll have to start all over again.

(It's like taking an axe to an apple tree — there will be no more apples.
And you'll have to plant a new tiny tree and wait years until it grows.)

I wowed my class!
by Eden

AGE: **8**

WHERE: **New South Wales**

My sister, Ella, and I do the jam jars at home, but my mum added another jar, called GROW. Each time we get to $100 we invest it in shares via an investing app that makes our money grow.

One day in class we were learning about budgeting, and I explained how I save my pocket money and that we have an extra jar and invest our money. The teacher thought I was so smart because it's something most grown-ups find hard to do, but it's just normal in our house.

❝ Because I am an investor, people think I'm really smart with money! ❞

How to set up your GROW bucket in 15 minutes flat!

I'm guessing you're very excited about setting up your **GROW** bucket, right?

Well, it's actually very easy to do.

It's as simple as signing up to **an investing app**, and letting the experts do the investing for you.

A big part of being a smart Barefoot Kid is doing your own research. There are heaps of investing apps to choose from, so let me take you through five simple steps that'll help you choose one that's right for you. Here's what you've got to do:

 1 **Make your parents a nice cold drink**

You'll need an adult to open the investment app account for you (the official term is 'as trustee'). So go and make them a cold drink, and let them know it won't take long!

You'll need these three things to open an account

1. your parent's permission

2. your parent's bank account details so they can transfer the money

3. proof of ID (your birth certificate, passport, or Medicare card).

2 **Google 'best investing apps for kids'**

You should be able to find *at least* five investing apps for kids. Write them down.

3 Check the minimums

Most apps will allow you to open an account with between $5 and $50, and then allow you to add some money each time you get paid (weekly, monthly, quarterly, or even one-off amounts).

4 Check the fee

Many investing apps for kids charge weekly or monthly fees (they're usually a few dollars). The problem is these fees will chew up your **GROW** bucket money like a worm eating an apple! So go with an app that does **not** charge these fees. This is very important!

5 Look at your options

Finally, once you've set up your app, it'll ask you to choose an investment option. The options usually have funny names like 'Conservative' or 'Balanced' or 'Growth'. Your money will generally grow faster in 'Growth', but you should only choose this if you're going to hold onto your shares for at least 10 years.

That's it!

In less than 15 minutes you're now officially an investor!

Go for growth!

The longer you can leave your money in your **GROW** bucket, the more your money will grow.

So whatever investment option you choose, don't forget the golden rule:

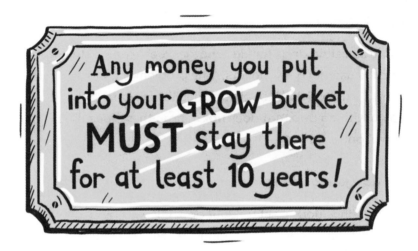

Why?

Because you need to give your apple tree a chance to grow.

Sometimes shares will go down — which is quite normal — and when that happens it can be scary. Yet the worst thing you could do is get scared and sell your shares — it's like chopping down your tree!

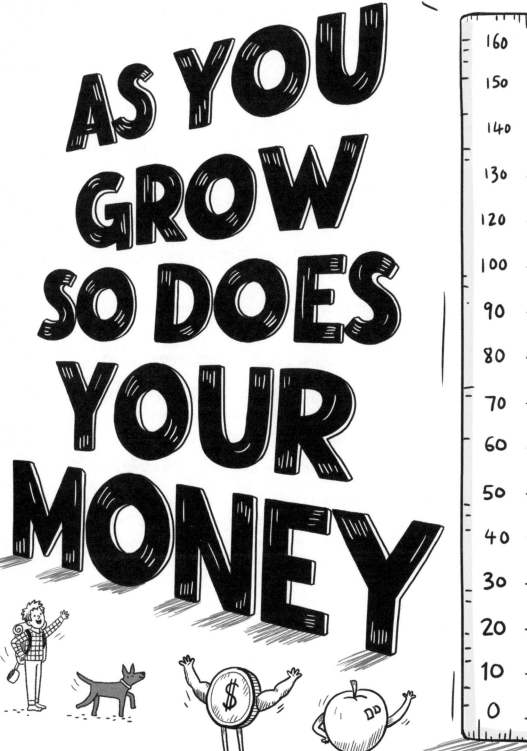

But I want to spend my money NOW!

The rule is that each bucket gets at least *some* money each payday. So if you want to spend some money now, take it from your SPLURGE bucket.

Trust me on this one, setting up your GROW bucket (and leaving your money in it) is one of the smartest things you'll ever do.

How much do I need to kick off my GROW bucket and start investing?

You can start with as little as $5! And you can set the app to automatically invest $5 (or more) each month.

How long do I have to hold my shares in my GROW bucket?

The longer you leave the shares in your GROW bucket, the bigger they grow. It takes 10 years to grow a decent-sized apple tree. Why would you want to chop it down early?

Should I just invest in the businesses that I'm interested in?

No. I like to own all the biggest shares in Australia and around the world — in one swipe of an investing app. The fancy name for this is an 'index fund', and it's the best place to grow your money. Most investing apps only offer index funds.

My parents say the share market is risky.

Most grown-ups didn't learn how to grow their money until they were much, much older. They didn't have a book like this when they were a kid to encourage them to plant their apple tree early . . .

Remember we talked about a grown-up yelling at the little tree trying to make it grow?

That doesn't work!

Yet if you plant an apple tree and forget about it, you can confidently come back years later and be drowning in apples. It's the same with the shares in your GROW bucket.

In fact, this is *another* reason you should set up your **GROW** bucket: you might be able to teach your parents how cool investing is!

How do I get money from shares?

Remember, you're becoming an owner in businesses. When they make money they either share some of that cash with you, the owner, (it's called a 'dividend'), or they use it to grow the business, which makes the share price go up.

How do I sell?

Well you don't need to think about that for Y-E-A-R-S. However, it's very easy — with most investing apps you just hit 'sell' instead of 'buy' and the money will be paid into your linked bank account a couple of days later.

I'm helping my mum learn about shares!

by Madison

AGE: 8

WHERE: Queensland

It's just me and Mum [Leona] at home, and she works really, really hard. When I told Mum that I wanted to set up a GROW bucket and invest in shares, she said she'd always wanted to buy shares but had no idea how to do it. She said she never learnt anything about it at school. We are now set up on an investing app. It's so cool that Mum and I can learn about investing in shares together!

> **I said to Mum, 'Don't worry, I think investing is pretty easy.'**

I'm an investing CHOCOHOLIC!
by Annie-Maree

AGE: **13**

WHERE: **New South Wales**

I didn't want to invest at first because I wanted to hold on to my savings. But then I realised having savings was good but growing my money was even better!

The way I look at it, you can save and buy a chunk of chocolate but it's heaps sweeter to own a chunk of the chocolate factory and you end up with a much bigger chocolate budget later on. One day I want to have enough money to fix things that we can make better in the world. I don't really want be to rich but I do want plenty of spare money so that if I see a person in need or a cause I believe in that needs money, I can afford to help them.

> **If you invest some of your savings as a kid, your wealth grows up with you.**

One last thing before you're done!

Do me a favour . . . put the book down, head to the kitchen and see if you have any nice crisp apples. Grab one and start munching on it while you give this **GROW** bucket quiz a go.

Circle the correct answers ↳

How much do you need to start investing in shares?

a $5
b $100
c $1000

Complete this sentence: The longer you leave shares, the . . .

a smaller they shrink
b bigger they grow
c more apple pies you get

What happens if you sell your shares and spend all the money in your GROW bucket?

a Nothing, it just keeps growing!
b You'll have to start all over again
c Worms will eat your apples

Why bother putting money in your GROW bucket?

a So you grow a little richer each day
b So you can one day buy big things like a car or a house, and look after your family
c Both of the above

ANSWERS: (c), (b), (b), (c)

CONGRATULATIONS!
YOU ARE A SHARE OWNING
SUPERSTAR!

This step has been about how you can grow your money.

However, let me tell you a little secret that I've learned from lots of Barefoot Kids:

✓ Your GROW bucket also massively grows your confidence.

✓ You will feel smarter, and cooler, because you're doing something that most grown-ups don't know how to do!

✓ Not only that, but you've made it through all the Barefoot Steps!

Go to the back of the book and get this sticker:

Stick it on the chart on page 23.

WELL DONE!

You're doing amazing things. Your apple tree is planted and it's growing strong, and so are you.

You're now part of a very cool club.

BAREFOOT STEPS
ON ONE PAGE

STEP 1
EARN SOME MONEY

STEP 2
STASH YOUR CASH

STEP 3
BE A BAREFOOT BOSS

STEP 4
GET WHAT YOU WANT

STEP 5
MAKE SOMEONE SMILE

STEP 6
GROW YOUR MONEY

Welcome, Barefoot Kid!

You made it!

I am so impressed.

Not everyone has made it to the end of this book — but you have!

Most people don't end up getting what they want — but you will!

Because you have been on the same **EPIC** adventure as the kids you've met in this book.

Here's what will happen for you next:

People are going to see what you're doing. They're going to notice that you're no ordinary kid.

You're going to be seen as the smart one . . . the one who is good with money.

Pretty soon, people will start looking at you differently, just like they did with Levi, who we met right back at the start of the book.

And YOU will start to look at yourself differently.

That's because you *are* different:

You are now a
BAREFOOT KID!

There's one final thing that will bring everything together . . .

It's official!

In most shops or businesses, you'll see a certificate on the wall.

It says they're for real, and licensed to do business.

Well, I've created a certificate just for you.

I want you to scan the QR code below. Once you've downloaded your certificate, fill it out and put it on display. Include it if you have a stall, put it on your website, use it as part of your marketing – wherever you are doing business, let people see you know what you're doing!

The certificate instantly tells your customers:

- ⭐ who you are
- ⭐ what you're doing
- ⭐ what you're saving for
- ⭐ how you will make a difference.

Your Barefoot Kids certificate tells the world that you are on an epic money adventure.

I HAVE ONE LAST TRICK. SCAN THIS TO GET A PRINTABLE COPY OF THE CERTIFICATE TO SHOW OFF TO YOUR FRIENDS AND YOUR CUSTOMERS!

BAREFOOT KIDS

CERTIFICATE

HELLO!

My name is .... and I'm .... years old.

My business is called ....

What I do is ....

I'M A HARD-WORKING BAREFOOT KID!

The money I earn is split four ways:

I keep a little to treat myself for my hard work.

I give some of my profits to .... because I care

about ....

I save for ....

I invest 10% of my profits into the share market
and earn compound interest every day.

TREAD YOUR OWN PATH!

THANK YOU

for supporting my business!

Can you please do me a favour?

You are now an influencer.

People are going to see what you're doing and wonder how you learnt to be so smart with money.

And so now I've got a favour to ask *you*:

Please show this book to three of your friends.

You'll be doing them a huge favour. After all, most kids still don't learn this stuff.

YOU can be responsible for getting your friends started on their own **EPIC money adventure**, helping them get what they want, and changing their entire life.

Please spread the word. It's the ultimate act of kindness!

THANK YOU!

NOW GO GET WHAT YOU *REALLY* WANT!

FUTURE
THIS WAY

In case you missed it!

Here are a few things you might want to read again while you're getting started.

Barefoot Kids in the book

The 'Barefoot' device is a trademark of The Barefoot Investor and is used under license by HarperCollins*Publishers* Australia

HarperCollinsPublishers
Australia • Brazil • Canada • France • Germany • Holland • India
Italy • Japan • Mexico • New Zealand • Poland • Spain • Sweden
Switzerland • United Kingdom • United States of America

HarperCollins acknowledges the Traditional Custodians
of the land upon which we live and work, and pays respect
to Elders past and present.

First published in Australia in 2022
by HarperCollins*Publishers* Australia Pty Limited
Gadigal Country
Level 13, 201 Elizabeth Street, Sydney NSW 2000
ABN 36 009 913 517
harpercollins.com.au

Copyright © Scott Pape and related entities 2022
Illustrations © Richard Watson 2022
Photographs © the contributors

The right of Scott Pape to be identified as the author of this work has been asserted by him in accordance
with the *Copyright Amendment (Moral Rights) Act 2000*.

This work is copyright. Apart from any use as permitted under the *Copyright Act 1968*, no part may
be reproduced, copied, scanned, stored in a retrieval system, recorded, or transmitted, in any form or
by any means, without the prior written permission of the publisher.

A catalogue record for this book is available from the National Library of Australia

ISBN 978 1 4607 6365 0 (paperback)
ISBN 978 1 4607 1601 4 (ebook)

Cover illustrations by Richard Watson
Art direction by Scott Pape
Photographs by the kids and their families unless otherwise stated
Printed by IVE

Disclaimer

The information in this publication is in the nature of general commentary only and has been prepared for
education purposes. It should not be construed as professional advice. It is not intended to provide specific
guidance for particular circumstances and it should not be relied on as the basis for any decision to take action
or not take action on any matter which it covers. Readers should obtain their own professional advice where
appropriate, before making any such decision.

The author is not affiliated with and does not endorse any of the corporate entities mentioned in or involved in
the distribution of this work, or any third party entities whose trademarks and logos may appear on this work.

Where the author discusses financial products or features of products it is for the purpose of educating readers.
The author does not take money or any other benefits from any product providers referred to in the publication.

To the maximum extent permitted by law, the author and publisher disclaim all responsibility and liability to
any person, arising directly or indirectly from any person taking or not taking action based on the information
in this publication.

Get This Book in YOUR School

Dear Primary School Educators,
If you are interested in purchasing class sets, please contact your education supplier.
Visit teachershub.com.au for teacher notes/classroom resources to accompany
this book.

BOSS

TREAD YOUR OWN PATH!

GOOD AS NEW

THAT'S PAWSOME!

BE THE BOSS!

APPROVED

Jump into the S.E.A.
Smile
Eye contact
Ask questions

APPROVED

BAREFOOT BOSS

HELLO
MY NAME IS

PAID

I'M A BAREFOOT KID!

PAID

1. I will make my bed every morning.
2. I will clear my dishes after every meal.
3. I will put my clothes in the laundry basket when I take them off.